From Vision to Decision

From Vision to Decision

A Self-Coaching Guide to Starting a New Business

Dana K. Dwyer

From Vision to Decision: A Self-Coaching Guide to Starting a New Business

Copyright © Business Expert Press, LLC, 2019.

Cover Image Credit: Pasuwan/Shutterstock.com

First published in 2019 by
Business Expert Press, LLC
222 East 46th Street, New York, NY 10017
www.businessexpertpress.com

ISBN-13: 978-1-94999-156-7 (paperback)
ISBN-13: 978-1-94999-157-4 (e-book)

Business Expert Press Entrepreneurship and Small Business Management Collection

Collection ISSN: 1946-5653 (print)
Collection ISSN: 1946-5661 (electronic)

Cover and interior design by Exeter Premedia Services Private Ltd., Chennai, India

First edition: 2019

10 9 8 7 6 5 4 3 2 1

Printed in the United States of America.

Abstract

Do you feel that you are called to be an entrepreneur but hesitate because you are just beginning and do not know what to do?

This book will help you find your way through the small business startup maze in order to build a small business that will support your dreams for a life full of meaning, joy, and profit. The self-coaching exercises in this book are designed to move you from a frustrated dreamer to becoming an action-oriented entrepreneur and business leader.

The focus of this self-coaching guide to building a profitable business is on your lifestyle—defining it, creating it, and ultimately sustaining it with the profits from your business.

Money cannot buy you happiness, but a solid, profitable business can enable you to wake up each morning looking forward to the work you have to do that day. It can fill your days with people you enjoy and people who value you and what you have to offer—people who willingly support you so you can continue to serve them with your product or service.

If you dream of owning your own small business because you want autonomy, freedom, meaning, and purpose, this book is for you.

Keywords

entrepreneur; business startup; lifestyle; money; happiness; wealth building; lifestyle business; business coaching; profitable business; self-coaching

Contents

Prepublication Reviews

As an entrepreneur your biggest job is dealing with yourself, knowing yourself, your ego, your emotions and your positive and negative attributes. This book will systematically walk you through the maze and chaos to success. The examples and quotes throughout clarify the issues. Doing the work chapter by chapter will serve you well and pay off in the end.

—Julia Rux, PhD, Developmental Psychology

Dwyer takes the fear out of starting your own business by taking you step by step through the stages needed to get your business launched. She covers everything from breaking the myths of owning your own business, to taking inventory of your deep desires, skills and strengths, to turning your vision into a profitable business. She even shows you how to manage your business once it is launched, and how to measure its success. Her disarming wit and no-nonsense approach will keep you engaged and moving toward your goals. As a seasoned entrepreneur, she knows how to avoid pitfalls and how to handle success and, like a great coach, often shares her wisdom through asking provocative questions like 'What are You Afraid of?,' 'Why Should People Give You Money?,' 'What Insulates You from Your Competitors?' Then, with questions in hand, she provides you with the tools you need to find the answers, which equips you to keep moving forward. Unlike other business-building authors out there, Dwyer befriends you, believes in you, and doesn't hold back. If you're looking for an engaging, easy-to-read resource with comprehensive, step-by-step instructions for getting your business launched, 'From Vision to Decision' is all you need.

—Jodi Q Hill, Digital Nomad

Preface

As I was completing the final chapter of this book, I came across a new (to me) personal assessment that claimed my "primary core value energy" is wisdom. In this case, wisdom is the ability to see the way things are and be able to discern what to do about it. To translate this definition of wisdom into my own terms, wisdom is the ability to honestly evaluate one's current reality and develop a creative strategy to move that reality closer to one's vision.

My secondary core value energy is love. In this sense, love is working toward an inspired vision of what can be by nurturing the core values in others.

I was struck by how my efforts to write this book have unconsciously demonstrated these innate, core-value energies of my life.

I hope this book has successfully shared whatever wisdom I possess with those who can benefit from it. I also hope I have helped you find an inspired vision of what can be, and that I have given you valuable tools to help you nurture your own core values. Most of all, I hope we—you and I—have built a relationship, and that things in this book and in the workbook training materials have helped you and your business thrive and flourish … that is my wish.

Introduction

I was not designed to be forced. I will breathe after my own fashion.
Let us see who is the strongest.

—Henry David Thoreau

Are you innovative, creative, and restless? Can you envision a life full of joy and meaningful activity that includes both work and love? Do you fantasize about quitting your job? Do you feel that you are called to be an entrepreneur but hesitate because you do not know where to start? Perhaps you have already started but feel confused about your next steps.

If so, you have come to the right place. This book is a thinking person's guide to help you think your way through the maze in order to build a business that will embody your dreams for a rich life full of meaning and joy. The self-coaching exercises contained in the book and in the supplemental workbook materials are designed to move you from being a visionary to being a strategizing and action-oriented entrepreneur.

The focus in this guide to building a profitable business is on your lifestyle—defining it, creating it, and ultimately sustaining it with the profits from your business.

I will tell you up front, if your vision is to be the next young business genius and your dream is to take the world by storm, this book will disappoint you. Some entrepreneurs want the excitement and adrenaline rush of big risks that might result in big rewards. If this is you and you are willing to work hard and have the grit to take those big risks, there are teachers out there who share your drive.

I know how that game is played. I studied under several high-powered wealth gurus and I played that game for years. Playing at that level caused me many sleepless nights. I made and ultimately lost a lot of money before I admitted to myself that adrenaline is *not* my substance of choice. Once upon a time, I wanted to be rich but now I understand true wealth as something other than a number on a spreadsheet. I believe money is only useful as a way to support a life of happiness. However, I do believe that the *process* of making money and the work involved in producing something of value can indeed create happiness. This book is about finding and then creating the business that will successfully create a life of happiness for you.

Money cannot buy you happiness, but a solid, profitable business can enable you to wake up each morning looking forward to the work you have to do that day. It can fill your days with people you enjoy and people who value you and what you have to offer—people who willingly support you so you can continue to serve them with your product or service.

If you dream of owning your own business because you want autonomy, freedom, meaning, and purpose, I am talking to you. If you hope to design and build a business that will release you from corporate servitude and allow you to live a fabulous life (*as defined by you—not by someone else!*), this book is for you.

Building a business is a process, and everyone doing so is at a different stage of the process. You may be at the point where you need to discover a great idea and figure out a clear plan for creating a new business that is unique to you. If so, you will find the exercises provided in this book will help you discover a business that is just right for you.

You may already have a powerful idea for your business, but you need the skills to develop it. You may need to create efficient systems and processes that synchronize with your idea. Thinking through the topics outlined here and in the workbook exercises will help you clarify your priorities, establish an action plan, and take concrete steps to build the business you can imagine.

On the other hand, you may already be working in your own small business, and perhaps you have discovered that success at any level comes with its own challenges. If your business is up and running, you may be ready to develop the skills of a business leader. Following the thinking process outlined in this book will take you from merely being self-employed, where you wear all the hats of the business and do all the work, to business leadership where your business becomes a system that can run without you.

Planning to Plan

I have been accused of planning how to plan, then progressing to plan, which then turns into plans of how to implement those plans. I do understand the temptation to stay safely stuck in the planning process, but that is *not* what this book is about. This book is about preparation, but you *will* go beyond that and get to the necessary action involved with building a business. The sooner you complete the thinking processes outlined here, the sooner you will be ready to take powerful, results-oriented steps toward your business success. If you skip this process, you may find yourself running on a treadmill—working hard but not really going anywhere. By reading and working your way through this book, you will know whether or not what you are planning will work long before you invest significant time, energy, and resources into your business idea.

Your business is just waiting to be created so, by all means, get into action! Take your first powerful step toward the entrepreneurial lifestyle of your dreams by creating a powerful plan.

Let us begin your entrepreneurial journey by sorting out the truth from fiction.

The Myths of Entrepreneurship

Myth #1—Entrepreneurs Are Doers, Not Thinkers

Thinking is always step one. You need to get into action, but first start by thinking. Entrepreneurs who head into action without a plan are indeed busy, but not necessarily *productive*. Being busy is a state that feeds the ego and may impress your friends, but when it is not productive, busyness leads to burnout and possible failure.

Myth #2—Entrepreneurs Are Born, Not Made

While it is true that entrepreneurs need characteristics like self-motivation, analytical ability, and vision, these traits are not genetic—they are learned. This book will help you recognize, clarify, adopt, and implement the characteristics you need in order to succeed, and it all begins with your thinking.

Myth #3—It Takes Luck to Succeed in Business

Let us face it, unless you grew up in a family of successful entrepreneurs, you never learned how to build a business. In most countries, education systems are designed to turn out good employees. The socialization of schoolchildren includes working well with others, following directions, competitiveness, and a complacent willingness to fit into a preordained, social hierarchy.

Few schoolchildren are encouraged to be innovative, independent, and act as a maverick, and often these tendencies are discouraged. As adults with these same tendencies and working in traditional jobs, we may find our biases toward independent decision making, creative problem solving, and boat-rocking innovation rarely nurtured in organizational environments.

This almost universal focus on "good jobs" leaves those individuals with creative entrepreneurial ideas devoid of the practical, business-creation skills they need in order to mold their ideas into real world businesses.

If you desire to be an entrepreneur, believe in yourself! Do not let the expectations of others stop you. You have ideas and you have the desire. What you need is a plan to help you develop your idea into a profitable business, and this book will supply just that as well as a new personal skill set—business leadership.

In this book, I have distilled the thought processes of a powerful business creator into a process-driven system. All you have to do to create a clear, low-risk plan for a profitable business is to *think*.

Myth #4—Thinking Is Easy

Thinking is hard work, but thinking is how we create. Whether you want to create a game-changing business model, create new innovations in an untapped market, or create yourself as an emerging entrepreneur, your first task is to think—a simple task, but not an easy one.

In this book, you will discover a process for thinking through all the potential pitfalls and challenges of your potential business, and you will think through your possible responses. When you have thought through all 10 chapters, you will have a solid model for a successful business.

This thinking process alone will put you light years ahead of most emerging entrepreneurs who begin with high hopes and no plan then end up in a J.O.B. situation.

J.O.B stands for "Just Over Broke." You do not really have a thriving business, but you can claim "success" because you are technically your own boss. Would-be entrepreneurs often begin on their own because they know how to do a certain task well, and they do not like working for someone else. The trouble with this plan, where the owner is also the sole employee, is there is a limit to available working hours that, in turn, limits the money to be made. A J.O.B. business often results in challenges and struggles that never end, together with worries that keep you awake at night—and that really is not very profitable.

Once you have thought your way through each of these topics, you will have a clear idea of the business you are building, specific expectations of the profits you can anticipate, as well as the lifestyle you will have, AND you will have invested only time and energy. You will have risked nothing beyond the money you spent to purchase this book.

Who Am I to Tell You How to Think?

If that thought has crossed your mind as you have been reading this book, I understand. You are, or you want to be, an entrepreneur and that independent spirit is part of your gift. I get it, and I respect it. So, let me tell you my story...

There was a time when I traveled to a corporate job each and every day. My weeks seemed to evaporate into thin air with a lack of significant meaning. I sat in traffic for an hour, each morning and evening, thinking, "I hate this job! This is no way to live my life!"

If you are familiar with the idea that our thoughts attract what we think about, both good and bad, then you will understand when I tell you that because I wanted to be free, I eventually found myself unemployed. Of course, because my intention was determined by negative thoughts, the reality was painful—I was involuntarily separated from my job. Unemployment was *not* what I had in mind. Without my hated job, I found myself with nowhere to go each day ... but at least I was out of the traffic! However, I was very much afraid for my future.

The upside was I had plenty of time to think.

At some level, I knew I wanted to have a lifestyle that would give me freedom and a meaningful life, but my fear kept me trapped in the same old solutions. Unable to think outside the "career" box, I made several wrong decisions. These decisions not only wasted my time but also caused me more misery and further undermined my self-worth. Do not worry—I will go into more detail about some of those wrong decisions later in the book. It was actually the pain of these wrong decisions that finally helped me make the changes I needed to make.

But for now, let me go on. When I saw my job disappear for the second time in two years (and I can still feel the emotional pain of that separation even as I write this), I finally started to think differently.

Leap, and the net will appear.

—John Burroughs

What changed my thinking was an inner commitment *never* to work another corporate job.

When I made that sincere and frankly desperate declaration to myself, I did not know *how* I would be able to accomplish that feat. I only knew that finally, I was willing to do whatever it would take to find a path that would suit me. Me ... the real me ... the me that did not fit into the corporate culture with all of my gifts, talents, abilities, interests, and desires.

Once I declared I would never take another corporate job, I set about considering my real needs and wants.

I realized that what I wanted was not the security of another job. What I really wanted was adequate income, work I enjoyed, and the freedom to live a life of meaning. What I wanted was not riches or piles of money, but rather a way to support the happy life I was imagining.

What I clearly recognized as the life I really wanted is what we call "vision." I was able to stop focusing on my negative, fear-based vision of becoming a lonely and forgotten bag lady. I came to understand my fear-based vision was no more real than my timid vision of possible success. I had been working hard just to *avoid* one possible negative outcome. When I began to think differently and could recognize what I really wanted, I was then able to start working *toward* something good instead of mere avoidance of something bad.

This change in my perspective expanded my creative options. When the focus is on just *avoiding* a negative outcome, there are only so many solutions. However, when the focus is on working *toward* something positive, there are many possible pathways to get there.

When I realized I wanted autonomy, adventure, and an income more than I wanted the security of a job, that was the moment when I became an entrepreneur. Well, I actually became an entrepreneur in mind only as I did not even have a business idea … yet.

> *The journey of a thousand miles begins with one step.*
>
> —Lao Tzu

It did not happen overnight. It truly was a journey, but it actually turned out to be a journey that I loved. With my new entrepreneurial self-image in mind, I set out to acquire mentors and teachers who taught me general business skills along with a great deal about myself. Over the next few years, I built, profited from, and sold several businesses all with the intention of fulfilling my desire of being able to live and work autonomously while using my gifts and traveling at the same time.

Look at Me Now

Look at me now. Although I am not Bill Gates, Steve Jobs, or Richard Branson, I *am* successful in ways that make me happy. I have an adventurous spirit, an analytical mind, a love of learning, and a tendency to hoard information—particularly information about building a business. I now recognize these things as my own personal gifts, and I believe my purpose in life is to share these gifts.

These days it is not only my calling but also my business model to share what I know with people who are just beginning their entrepreneurial journey. What I know is how to teach the skills you need in order to create a profitable business.

I was once afraid and ignorant, and if I can reinvent myself as a successful entrepreneur, so can you!

Who Is This Book for

As you probably can tell from my story, I am not going to push you to dominate your market, crush your competition, or build an empire—unless that is what you want to do as part of your business plan.

These days many business start-up books are written for a self-styled and elite group of "geeks" who eventually aim to seek venture capital cash. This young, well-educated, and well-connected crowd often sneers at what they refer to as "lifestyle" businesses, but a lifestyle business is exactly what this book is specifically designed to help you develop.

In fact, even if world domination appeals to you, I would still suggest that you start with this book. You will need an income to sustain you while building your empire. The skills you learn as you build your first business will serve you well with all your future endeavors in the years to come.

Enjoyment is not a goal; it is a feeling that accompanies important ongoing activity.

—Paul Goodman

Are you ready? Let us get started …

What Is in This Book

In this book, you will learn:

How to Overcome Your Biggest Barrier to Entering the Market. It is human nature to fear the unknown. The key to changing into the entrepreneur you want to be is to feel the fear but do it anyway. The good news is there are techniques to help you do this.

Getting Started Right—Envision What You Want. Knowing what you really want is often the hardest part of this process. It may be hard, but it is important because when you are clear, you will become motivated to move forward.

Vision and Current Reality—Which Business Is Right for You? If you *want* to be an entrepreneur, you already have the calling to be one. What you know and who you are—these things hold the keys to your first (or next) powerful business idea.

Crafting A Business Vision From Your Mission. The difference between creating a J.O.B. for yourself and building a profitable business lies in the planning. Thinking hard enough to find the answers to a few critical questions can actually make the difference between success and failure.

Turning Your Business Vision Into a Profitable Business Model. Never forget your business is a system intended to create value. Your business model is a clear picture of the exchange where you add value to the raw product, and the market gives another value—money—in exchange.

Owning Your Own Business—Strategy and Objectives. The strategies you choose to use in order to accomplish your objectives will define the work you do each day. It is important to choose strategies that will allow you to live a meaningful life in the present moment while you are working toward your goals for the future.

How to Finance Your Brilliant Idea. Your goal as an entrepreneur is not to borrow money but to build a business that can be proven by performance. You need to show potential investors that you can indeed make *more* money over and above what they are investing in your business. When you can show that, the money will come to you.

How to Know if Your Business Is a Success. No matter the size of your business or your intentions, you will not succeed—at least not in any sustainable way—until you have analyzed the numbers for your eventual success. If you spend some time thinking clearly about what statistics would show success, you will know where you are going. You will also have some specific numbers to alert you that you actually have arrived at the place you intended to go with your business.

Action Planning—How to Do the Right Thing. When movement is the only criteria for action, the daily task list can collapse into chaos. Managing chaos every day has its ego-related rewards but, in most cases, the rewards are not monetary, long lasting, or productive. Creating a specific task plan and managing it well is the key to success.

Chaos Theory—Preparing for the Future. A system is anything that is not chaos. Your business, as you now conceive it, is a system. As a system, it is dynamic. It *will* change. You need to be prepared to adapt to that change.

Who Are You Now? One day you will stop, look around, and realize you have indeed created your vision. What will you do then?

How to Get the Most From This Book

This is a self-coaching guide intended to help you think. If you read it from cover to cover but do not stop to think, you will have missed the value. If you skip the valuable exercises—both the ones contained in this book as well as the additional tools available in the workbook—you will have wasted your time.

If you savor the process ... if you stop to think ... if you write down your thinking and ultimately organize your thoughts into a simple, one-page business plan with a vision, mission, objectives, strategies, and action steps, you will have everything you need to get your business off the ground.

CHAPTER 1

How to Overcome Your Biggest Barrier to Entering the Market

One-third of emerging entrepreneurs decided they wanted to be entrepreneurs BEFORE they had a brilliant business idea. This was certainly true for me. I did not know *how* to be in business for myself. I just knew working in a corporate cubicle was turning me into a frightened and worried failure. My "aha" moment came when I realized what I really wanted was *not* the security of another job with a bigger desk. What I *really* wanted was to be free to pursue my own gifts. I came to understand that what was holding me back from the life I wanted was *not* a lack of money. My life was not how I really wanted it to be because of my own fears—fear of failure … fear of success … fear that I did not have what it would take … fear of being different … fear of the work involved … and countless other vague and imagined dangers.

Most of my fears were contained in a deep-seated dread that if I went to work for myself, I would not have enough money.

That fear is a common one … it is also more or less irrational.

Fear Is Human Nature—What Are You Afraid of?

It is said that almost half of American women fear they will become "bag ladies" someday. Even Oprah Winfrey, whose net worth may be as much as $1.5 billion, once told a reporter she had $50 million in cash socked away as her "bag-lady fund." If women fear failure, and dread being alone and without resources, men are also afraid of failing: losing status, inviting criticism, being powerless and broke.

These fears loom large when one begins to consider starting a business.

I know how real the fear feels and how dangerous it can be. I meet with aspiring entrepreneurs every week. Some are young and stuck in boring, low-status jobs. From their cubicles where they while away their time each day, they see their youthful dreams of greatness and success slipping away. Others are looking to balance life, love, and earning an income. Young women are usually hoping to start a family and men want to provide more for their children. All of them have the calling to become an entrepreneur but, after meeting with me, many of them—most in fact—go away and never take the first step. They tell me the challenge is money, but money is really just an excuse. The real challenge is their own fear.

> *Ultimately, we know deeply that the other side of every fear is freedom.*
> —Marilyn Ferguson

As you contemplate leaving behind the safe, secure role you have been trained to fill—the role of a hardworking, secure employee, one assured of his social standing and of a steady paycheck—there truly *is* a lot to be afraid of.

According to David Rock, CEO of Results Coaching Systems International (one of my teachers), much of our human behavior is driven by our deep desire to minimize threat while maximizing reward.

Minimizing Threats

This desire to minimize threat is primitive. The same part of our brain that generations ago scanned the grasslands for lions now scans our social environment for possible threats. When a threat is perceived, this small part of the brain (called the amygdala) responds with the same ancient and primitive message our ancestors heard: React! Withdraw, retreat, contract—in other words, be afraid.

Maximizing Rewards

Our brains are also hard-wired to approach when there appears to be a possibility of reward: money, food, shelter, sex, or material goods. When we perceive a reward, we are, at a deep level, inclined to reach for it.

The catch is that this primitive and lightning fast part of our ancient survival mechanism is subconscious. We respond to our brain's primitive and unconscious assessment of situations as being either threatening or rewarding without being consciously aware of our motivations.

The mechanism we use to assess our environment has not evolved much beyond our hunting and gathering days. What has changed is the nature of our perceived rewards and threats.

According to David Rock (*SCARF: A Brain-Based Model for Collaborating With and Influencing Others, 2008*), our fears are now more often focused on our social experiences including status, certainty, autonomy, relatedness, and fairness. However, thanks to the vigilance of our older, more primitive brain, we respond to social threats with the same flight or fight circuitry we once used to run away from a threatening beast. A perceived threat to our status (or monetary security) activates the same network in our brain as a threat to our life. A positive event, social recognition or an increase in fairness, like a raise, activates the same neural networks as a reward.

When you begin seriously considering your future as an independent entrepreneur, you are entering territory rife with social threats. You are also entering a world rich with reward. Your brain is busy.

Threats to Status

Status is about our relative importance to others. Our sense of status goes up when we feel better than someone else does. An increase in status can feel similar to a financial windfall. Increasing one's status by creating a profitable business is a reward. It is one you are attracted to or you would not be reading this book.

However, a threat to one's status, as when one leaves a familiar and set hierarchical social group and sets out alone, is experienced in the brain in the same way we experience real physical pain. Thus, we fear failure as a threat to our very existence.

Threats to Certainty

Certainty is about our ability to recognize patterns and use this unconscious perception to predict the future. For example, when you pick up a cup of coffee you do not have to think about where to put your fingers to avoid being burned. Your brain has created and absorbed the pattern of picking up a cup of coffee. Your brain, without you being aware of it, is able to predict the pattern and adapt accordingly. If that familiar pattern is interrupted, say the cup is slippery, you will immediately pay conscious attention. Without this ability unconsciously to predict, your brain must use other, more demanding resources to process your in-the-moment experiences.

Any kind of significant change can generate uncertainty. Changing your focus from secure employment to business leadership will create a great deal of uncertainty.

The act of creating certainty out of uncertainty is rewarding and consequently something you will want to work toward. The exercises in the book will help you create certainty where now you may feel uncomfortably uncertain.

Threats to Autonomy

Autonomy is about our sense of having control over the events that will affect us. As humans we like to have choices. When we increase our perception of our own autonomy by leaving the corporate workforce, we feel rewarded.

When we feel we have little control, as in a dead-end job where one has little ability to influence outcomes, we feel a strong threat response.

Ask yourself this question: How much of your drive to become an entrepreneur is a result of your drive for autonomy?

Threat to Relatedness

Relatedness is about belonging or not belonging to a larger group. One of the advantages of working for an organization is you are related to a larger, familiar group by default.

When you strike out on your own, you will begin meeting new people. When confronted with strangers our brains quickly determine whether someone is "like us" or "unlike us." When we perceive someone as alike, our brains process information using circuits similar to those we use for our own thoughts. When we perceive someone as dissimilar, or a foe, different circuits are used.

As you set out to start a business, you may feel uncomfortable, perhaps even fearful of meeting strangers; this is due to your primitive brain's desire for safe, familiar human contact.

Threats to Fairness

Fairness is about the various types of fair exchanges between people in general. Unfair exchanges generate a strong threat response. People may feel strong emotions when confronted with perceived unfair behavior. Indeed, people have been known to die righting perceived injustices.

As you venture into a new arena that is often described as "cut-throat," you may have fears about the fairness you will (or will not) find in the world you are going to be part of.

To minimize the threat from potential unfairness you can establish clear expectations with measurable objectives and a shared vision. This book will help you do just that.

Be Afraid, Be Very Afraid

So you see, at some deep level, you (and your primitive brain) do not want to go into business. At some level, you just want to be comfortable and sure of yourself. If you change … if you become an entrepreneur or take risks to grow your business, you will almost certainly be uncomfortable and uncertain. Your primitive brain will be upset and, when your primitive brain is upset and sending you ever-increasing signals to be anxious and afraid, you will not think clearly.

> *Fear destroys the capacity to learn.*
>
> —Bruce Perry

In this state of fear, your brain will begin to scan for any threats to your status, certainty, autonomy, relatedness, and fairness. In addition, because of another hardwired feature of our human brains, the *reticular activating device* (RAS) to be exact, what you look for is most often what you will find.

Your RAS is a bundle of nerves at the base of your skull. This bundle of nerves has many functions, but it is most known for filtering out nonessential information (think traffic noise) and letting in information of significance. Consider the scenario of a city street, for instance. You probably will not really notice empty parking spaces unless you happen to be looking for one in order to park your car.

This ability to program your brain to see what you want to see is a two-sided coin. Proponents of the idea that we can manifest our desires encourage the clear and detailed visualization of what we want. The theory is by programming our brains to focus on what we want, we will activate our RAS to recognize an opportunity.

However, unfortunately, our RAS is more naturally adept at supporting our primitive brain's mandate to protect us from danger. Without conscious control, your natural fears will determine what your RAS lets in. For example, as you consider your potential to change, your fears will be paramount. You will begin to notice boarded-up storefronts. You will remember with humiliating immediacy your struggle with mathematics in school; you may imagine a future where your finances are ruined, your children are resentful, and your friends fade away. Your RAS will do its job by finding examples of all the dangers you can imagine, and you will find yourself in fight or flight mode.

Every week I meet with aspiring entrepreneurs who, when asked to step out of their comfort zone, give in to their fears and flee.

Courage is not the lack of fear but the ability to face it.
—Lt. John B. Putnam Jr.

Be Afraid, But Do It Anyway

The good news is there are ways to manage your fear. Knowing fear management techniques can help you throughout your journey to becoming an entrepreneur.

Fears Are Real, But You Can Manage Them

There is a definite and important difference between managing your fears and just plain ignoring them. I would guess that fear repression is a main coping mechanism of the 50 percent of business owners who fail in the first few years. If something about your business plan or the results you are getting is making you anxious and afraid, talk about it—look at the facts, assess the risk, and get help. Do all this before you decide to flee back to a J.O.B. The tools in this book will help you understand which fears belong to your current reality and which belong to your primitive brain.

Your fears *are* real but do not let them stop you. You can use the techniques described here to manage your emotional reactions and continue to move forward in spite of them—to be afraid and do it anyway.

Talk About It

Entrepreneurship, especially in the early days, can be a lonely business. Talking to someone about your fears and doubts will help calm you down. Neuroscientist Kevin Ochsner, Associate Professor and Director of Graduate Studies in the Department of Psychology at Columbia University, conducted an experiment where he showed test subjects an upsetting video. After they watched the video, he tested the participants for signs of psychological arousal. One group was instructed to talk about their feelings about being upset. Talking about their feelings in this group resulted in lower blood pressure among other benefits. Others were asked to suppress their emotions—to hide their feelings from other participants. The members of this group showed signs of being more upset with greater levels of psychological arousal.

It really does help to talk about it—the boogeyman under the bed is always bigger and scarier than the one exposed in the light.

Naming

One possible reason it helps to talk about our fears is the effect that naming fears and emotions can have on our brain. Studies have shown that the simple process of describing our feelings with words, and preferably words spoken aloud, has a healthy suppressing effect on our primitive brain. Naming your feelings will stop your primitive brain in its tracks, at least for the moment. Naming your uncomfortable feelings as fears and analyzing their root causes moves your emotional reaction up to your "higher" mind where you are able to choose your response instead of just automatically reacting.

Reappraisal

Every waking moment of every day, you and your primitive brain are making judgments about the events and circumstances of your life. The meaning you assign to these events and circumstances affects your reality, and your view of reality affects your subsequent actions. If you realize the meaning you assign to your experiences actually activates your fear mechanism, you can always reappraise the situation.

When you hear a noise in the night, your first appraisal (or the meaning you assign to the noise) can cause high levels of anxiety and fear. You may reach for a baseball bat or gun, and if you do, you run the risk of initiating dire consequences. When you reconsider enough to recognize the noise as just a door slamming in the wind, you have reappraised and your level of fear will (slowly) decrease.

There is nothing to fear but fear itself.

—Franklin D. Roosevelt

Clearly, your biggest barrier to entering the market, to becoming an independent, autonomous businessperson, is your very own brain-generated fear.

Awareness of what is going on in your brain, the ability to name your emotions, and being able to consciously choose to recognize the fear and do it anyway, are all tools you can use to help you take the first steps toward building your business idea into something great.

Next Steps

If you feel called to be an autonomous or more powerful businessperson but are hesitant to change your current status, you are exhibiting a common fear. Experiments show that the perception of status increases as people master a new skill. Acknowledge yourself for your entrepreneurial accomplishments.

If you are seeking more information to increase your level of certainty before you act, you are displaying caution. Uncertainty causes tension and discomfort. Use self-awareness to monitor your levels of uncertainty. Seek to maintain a level that will spark your curiosity and motivate you to solve problems.

If you are developing new relationships with clients, vendors, and staff, you will need to build trust carefully. Seek out opportunities to relate to others and avoid isolation. To your brain social isolation is similar to physical pain.

If you aim to create a business that will provide value in the marketplace *and* make a reasonable profit, you are honoring a universal sense of fairness.

When you have completed the exercises in this book, you will have done all you can to reduce your risks and assuage your fears. Then it will be time to move into purposeful and targeted action.

If you jump into business building without a well-thought-out plan, there is a very real threat to your survival—at least to your survival at the same level of comfort you and your loved ones now enjoy.

Your fear is real, but it does not need to be a showstopper. Here in your hands is the key to managing your fear. Now … before you leap, take the time to learn, take the time to do the brain-based work of creating a plan. The effort will help you gain emotional control, and in the process, you will build a solid model for a business that will set you free from the corporate grind.

The only limit to our realization of tomorrow will be our doubts of today.
—Franklin D. Roosevelt

The Self-Coaching Workbook

This is a self-coaching guide. If I was working with you one-on-one, I would ask you to reflect on the ideas we have discussed in each chapter. Since I am not with you, your willingness to do the following exercises and continue your learning will make all the difference in your success.

At the end of each chapter, you will find thinking exercises, tools to help you with your business analysis, techniques for greater creativity, additional information about your brain and how it works and powerful questions to lead you to a fuller understanding of yourself and your business.

Introduction: How to Use This Self-Coaching Workbook

The additional materials in this workbook are intended to be both a self-coaching guide and a resource of tools and techniques for taking your desire to build your own business from the idea stage to a clear, practical, and motivating plan.

To complete this process, you will need to do some careful thinking about who you are, what you want, and what you intend to create. You will also need to gather and analyze data and facts in order to make the best business decisions possible. For the best possible outcome, you will need to do these exercises with serious intent.

The tools are simple. You will need Internet access, writing materials, a notebook or online journal, a pen or word processing program, and a quiet place to think and write. Most importantly, you will need to commit to doing the hard work of thinking.

You will gain the most insight when you have read the appropriate chapter in the book before beginning the exercises.

Happy Thinking.

Module 1 Workbook

How to Overcome Your Biggest Barrier to Entering the Market

- Learn to manage the emotional side of embarking on a new and challenging journey.
- Recognize and name your fears.
- Reappraise your thoughts about your fears.
- Practice programming your RAS.

It is human nature to fear the unknown. The key to changing into the entrepreneur you desire to become is to acknowledge the fear—but do it anyway. The more you learn to recognize, understand, and control your natural emotional responses, the more prepared you will be to manage your behavior. The exercises in this lesson will give you the skills to recognize and manage your fears.

Information	Let Us Talk About It
Thinking/Writing	Name Your Fears
Thinking/Writing	Reappraisal
Visioning	How to Use Your RAS

Index to Exercises

Let Us Talk About It

In these online videos you will hear from academics and entrepreneurs about fear, what it can teach us, how to use it, and how to react when, as sometimes happens, our fears become real.

What Fear Can Teach Us	What if we thought about fear as an amazing link to the imagination? *Karen Thompson Walker, Author*
Turning Fear into Fuel	Let us talk about fear of failure, fear of judgment and fear of success *Jonathan Fields, Serial Entrepreneur*
A Kinder, Gentler Philosophy of Success	Are you absolutely sure the success you fear is the success you want? *Alain de Botton, Writer, Philosopher, and Presenter*
Courage to Fail	We cannot really talk about icons, geniuses and mavericks unless we talk about failure *Richard Sudek, Angel Investor*

Name Your Fears

Life is either a daring adventure or nothing.

—Helen Keller

WRITE IT DOWN

| |
| |
| |
| |

This is a thinking/writing exercise. Record both the positive and negative beliefs you hold about yourself. Use a notebook or word processing program to record your thoughtful answers to the following powerful questions:

- What do you believe about your ability to be a successful entrepreneur?
- What emotions do you feel when asked to acknowledge your belief in your potential?
- What emotions do you feel when asked to recognize and accept your weaknesses?

Writing is the doing part of thinking.

Reappraisal: What if You Did Not Believe Your Thoughts?

It is often said that your thoughts create your reality. It is wordier but more accurate to say your thoughts about your reality create your experience of that reality. Those thoughts may be unconscious, such as when your instinctual brain sounds a fight or flight alarm at the sound of a car backfiring. Your emotions, created from your memories, and the reality you have created out of past experience, color your thoughts about a situation. Your thoughts create your unique and individual perception of your in-the-moment reality.

But…just because you think it is true doesn't mean it *is* true. What if you did not believe your thoughts?

Recall your answer from the *Naming Your Fears* exercise on the previous page. *Now you will have a chance to reappraise your thoughts about those fears.*

WRITE IT DOWN

Think about the following questions. Write your responses down:

- Why do you believe these things?
- What in your past experience has influenced your thoughts?
- What if you are wrong? What if what you believe is not true?
- What if you are right? What if you fail? (Write out a realistic scenario—not Doomsday—realistic.)
- How will you recover?
- What if you do nothing? (Look out 5, 10, 15 years. Will you be better off?)
- What if you succeed?
- What does success feel like?

About Your Reticular Activating Systems (RAS)

Your *Reticular Activating System (RAS)* is a part of your brain that connects your conscious mind with your unconscious mind. The job of your RAS is to alert you to pay conscious attention to important information: for example, when your name comes up in a conversation. It also helps you filter out irrelevant information; traffic noise, other people's conversations—unless your name comes up.

What is important to the RAS, beside your survival, is *what you tell it is important*. When you decide what is important to you, your RAS will respond—literally. If you are considering buying a new phone, your RAS will draw your attention to people using the phone you are considering. Before your decision to purchase that particular phone, you may never have noticed how popular it was.

But beware. Your RAS is more of a computer than a friend. It will reinforce *whatever* you believe, and it cannot distinguish between a real event and an imagined event. If you believe you cannot start a business because you do not have what you need (money, time, skill, and connections), your RAS will notice and support your perceived lack "*whether it is true or not.*"

Your RAS only finds information that supports your beliefs. You tell your RAS what to look out for.

How to Use Your RAS

To program your RAS to help you achieve your chosen goals, you need to tell it to look for what you want. This is often referred to as "setting your intention" and often begins with an exercise in visioning.

What follows are instructions on how to create a powerful vision of what it is you want to create.

Note: I agree that this seems like a lot of instruction for something you probably do quite naturally but, as you move forward in the process of the creating your business, visioning will become a very important activity. Important not only for its value in programming your RAS but in its ability to help you to clarify exactly what it is you want to create. The more seriously you take this exercise, the more value you will find.

Visioning is important for your brain.

It is also important for your business.

Program Your RAS With a Vision

To begin, find a quiet place where you can relax and focus on your personal vision. You will be asked do this visioning process several times as you complete the exercises in this book. For this your first effort, you should just practice the technique. Practice now will improve your results later on.

Directions

Step 1: Relax. Relaxation and meditation are useful techniques for finding the proper mental space for your vision. If you do not usually meditate, you can just sit quietly for a few minutes concentrating on your breath. Do this until you feel a sense of inner quiet.

Step 2: Imagine you have accomplished all that you want most out of your life. Do not concern yourself with how possible or impossible this vision seems.

Step 3: Notice your point of view. Are you watching yourself on a screen? Are you the audience for your vision? This third person point of view is a common point of view.

Step 4: Revisit your vision but this time imagine it is happening right now. "I *have* a 40-foot sailboat," not "I *will have* a 40-foot sailboat." Make it as real and present as possible. View it from behind your own eyes. This is the first person, present tense point of view.

This real, present, first-person point of view vision is fodder for your RAS. When you are clear about your future reality, your RAS will set to work to find the information you need to create it.

Step 5: Revisit your vision one more time and enhance what you see, feel and smell. You are the director and you want this scene of your desired reality to be big, bold and inspiring. Enhance the color, the sound, and the smells. Make your vision as real as you possibly can.

WRITE IT DOWN

| |
| |
| |
| |

You have created your first vision. I hope you had fun. You will be revisiting this process many times. Have fun with it. Think big. Do not believe your negative thoughts. Just dream.

CHAPTER 2

Getting Started: Envision What You Want

If you limit your choices only to what seems possible or reasonable, you disconnect yourself from what you truly want, and all that is left is a compromise.

—Robert Fritz

Any creative process—and building your own business is definitely a creative process!—begins with vision.

If you are a rational, action-oriented person, you may be tempted to skip this chapter and go straight to the action steps, but as the Cheshire Cat famously said, "If you do not know where you are going, how will you know when you get there?" However, what is even more important is how will you know if what you are building is what you truly want?

Think of your business as your valuable contribution to the world. The purpose of your business is to create something of sufficient value that people will pay you for that something. However, your business is not only a business, but it is also your creative endeavor to live a life that is personally fulfilling. Often these two areas—work and life—conflict and compete for priority instead of working together to provide your ideal lifetime experience.

The key to figuring things out in the work/life arena is to use that conflict between work and life to create new solutions that will provide fulfillment in both areas.

Begin With the End in Mind

What do you *really* want? Envision what your "perfect" life would look like, and, if you have not already, create a rough draft of that life vision now.

Do not worry about whether your vision of an ideal life is "good" or "right" or whether your friends and family will approve. After all, it is *your* life, and this is just a rough draft of what you want your life to look like. As you work through the exercises in this book, your vision will change and grow—as it should. You may look back on the rough draft you are about to create and wonder what you were thinking. Then again, you might just be one of the lucky few who knows exactly what they want. Either way, writing out a life vision is beneficial for anyone and everyone.

What is your vision?

Ask yourself:

If time and money were no object and I could be anyone I want to be or do anything I want to do, or have everything I want, who would I be? What would I do? What would I have?

Be expansive and unrealistic, but be honest and true to yourself.

Write or type your answer in whatever manner you wish, but keep it readily accessible because you will want to revisit your thinking as you work through this book.

Rough Draft Vision #1

WRITE IT DOWN

You will also find this exercise in the workbook at the end of this chapter.

Recognize the Structure of Your Life

Your vision is *your* vision, and your life is *your* life.

No matter how you might prefer for your life to be, in reality your life is actually already happening. You already have interests, talents, experiences, and opinions. You already have people you love and people who love you. More than likely, you already have ex-lovers, children, pets, bills, friends, and enemies.

Your life experiences, your skills, your values, your responsibilities, both welcome and unwelcome, make up the configuration or structure of the life you are currently living. Just as a building has a steel frame or the configuration of an airplane includes wings, your life also has a certain structure. The configuration of your life is made up of those things that influence who you are and what, ultimately, you want.

Think of any structure as a whole thing made up of many different parts: a car, a blender, a university, are all structures made up of parts. When the parts are combined, they work together to accomplish a specific goal: movement, rotation, and learning.

The configuration determines the goal. Changing the outcomes determined by the structure is difficult, if not impossible. For example, an airplane's overall configuration is designed to provide a way for people to fly. Once you place yourself within the structure of the plane and it begins to fulfill its purpose, you have little choice but to sit back and enjoy the ride until the plane lands.

Your life is like that. Your life has a configuration of parts or structure that forms your identity. Some parts of your life support what you want to be and who you want to become, while other parts may hold you back. It can be difficult—very difficult—to figure out which parts of your structure you automatically adopted without thinking and, more importantly, which parts no longer serve the purpose of your life. As children, adults tell us what to believe, who to trust, what is important. When we are young, we naturally adopt this worldview and incorporate it as part of the configuration of our life. Now, as an adult seeking a meaningful and profitable life, it is important to question the ideas and values you have adopted merely by default. You must do this in order to be able to discover for yourself what you truly want for your own life or for your own business.

These two aspects of life, what you want (your vision) and what you already have (your current reality), are included in the structure of this book. As you work through these chapters, you will move back and forth between the vision of what you want for your future life and the reality of what your life is right now.

While recognizing exactly what your current reality is can be sobering, it is also the best place to start in order to build the life you want.

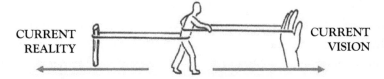

CURRENT
REALITY

CURRENT
VISION

Figure 2.1 Illustration of creative tension

Use Creative Tension to Your Advantage

When you know what you want on one hand while, on the other hand, you are aware and accepting of where you are in present reality, tension is created. I credit Robert Fritz, author of the *Path of Least Resistance: Learning to Become the Creative Force in Your Own Life*, with this idea as well as the preceding graphic (Figure 2.1) that describes it. I first discovered Fritz many years ago, and I use his concept of creative tension to motivate myself in many ways.

According to Fitz, tension is a fundamental component of the creative process.

> *There will always be tension in the beginning of the creative process, for there will always be a discrepancy between what you want and what you have. Why? Because creators bring into being creations that do not yet exist. In fact, part of your job as a creator is to form this tension.*
> —Robert Fitz

A few years ago, my reality at the time included an empty nest. I found myself working hard to maintain a house that was now too big for me, cooking food for a family that no longer came to the table and running my businesses on autopilot. In fact, even my dog was in failing health. Slowly, I came to recognize my feelings of dissatisfaction. My familiarity with the Fitz graphic shown earlier and his view of structures in our lives helped me frame my unhappiness because of the outdated structures in my current reality. I was living within the structure of mother, pet owner, business owner, when many of these roles no longer served a purpose.

Once I recognized the structures that were framing my life and realized those roles that were no longer meaningful, I was able to begin to create an entirely new reality for myself. With the unavoidable, and not necessarily welcomed, changes in my current reality came a chance to create a challenging and motivational vision of the *new* life I wanted to see become my new reality.

For me, the change I imagined and began to create was a move from suburban Virginia in the United States to South Africa. I realize such a major change is not everyone's cup of tea, but it was an exciting and growth-producing change of reality for *my* life.

Even though I had fantasized about traveling and living abroad for decades, it was not an easy change to accomplish. Once I committed to the vision, it took another two years to make the move a reality. In my case, natural life circumstances allowed for such a change.

For you, the tension between your current reality—where you are right now and your vision and where you want to be in the future—may be great. The effort and hard work needed to move toward your vision may seem tremendous. Your vision itself may make you uncomfortable. My vision of moving to Africa certainly made me uncomfortable. Nevertheless, even though the tension may be uncomfortable, that discomfort is a tool that can be used to your advantage. When you know exactly what you will need to overcome in order to move from your current reality to the new reality you want to create, you can make a realistic plan. And once you have a plan, all it takes is enough motivation to take a small step and move into action.

This book will provide the tools and guidance necessary to help you become very clear about your vision—your vision for your life and, more specifically, your vision for your business. Once you are clear about your vision, you will take a closer look at your present reality. When you know what is true about you, your life structure, and your values. When you know what is true about your market, your business model, and your finances, and you have acknowledged and addressed your personal strengths and weaknesses, you will then be in a position to address the tension you have created with a powerful action plan for creating the ultimate life you have envisioned.

We will look closely at all these things in the next few chapters, but for now, let's keep dreaming about your vision...

Your Vision

Unbelievably, becoming very clear about what you want as opposed to knowing what you *do not* want is often the hardest yet most important part of the creative process.

The business you set out to build for yourself must be designed to create the life you want, whether you are looking for wealth, fame, power, world peace or a steady income, or all of the aforementioned, while doing work that is both fulfilling and, at the same time, enjoyable. Depending on your current reality, you may need to start slowly by developing a small business venture to use as a stepping-stone to the knowledge and financial capital you will need to build your dream business and thus your dream life. Since the path you choose to follow to achieve what you want will be your creative life's work, it is important to begin the hard work by becoming clear on what kind of business you really want. And, in order to understand what you really want, you will first need to know why you want it.

I've come to know that what we want in life is the greatest indication of who we really are.

—Richard Paul Evans, The Gift

Money and Happiness

Does money make you happy? While a lack of needed cash can make you unhappy, stressed, anxious, and limit your freedom, how much money is enough to meet your needs and make you happy?

Many people, perhaps including yourself, might answer that question with, "as much as I can get." However, the science of positive psychology has found that happiness does not necessarily come from having money in and of itself.

Martin Seligman and the Institute for Positive Psychology have studied what it takes for people to become truly and sustainably happy, not just happy in a given moment. They discovered that lasting happiness actually comes from:

- Enjoying and being challenged by the work you do
- Having close relationships with family and friends
- Having good health
- Having a positive and optimistic outlook on life
- Having a strong belief in yourself

None of these lasting characteristics of happy people requires a large amount of cash, an investment portfolio, or multiple credit cards.

There is, however, a lower limit. If you have very little money over a long period, you will have a hard time maintaining the factors necessary for happiness. But ... having more than enough money will not, by itself, increase any of them.

To have a business that makes you truly wealthy, you not only need cash, but you also need good health, love, interesting work, a belief in yourself, and a positive outlook on life. Can you see how important it is for you to choose the right business *for you*? You need a business that will provide all the factors of happiness for yourself along with the income you need to live your ideal life.

So, let us start building your business by entering into an idea creation process. We will begin by developing a deeper self-understanding of who *you* are and what *you* bring to the marketplace.

Values

Values are personal beliefs and attitudes about the way you believe things should be. Groups, societies, and cultures all have particular values that are shared by their members. Your business should reflect not only your personal values but also those of the larger community of customers and employees you will be working with.

Deliberate and careful thinking about your own personal values, priorities, and motivational inner vision is important work, but beware you may find the thinking process to be a lot harder than it sounds.

It can be quite difficult for us to learn to think outside of the box, outside of the familiar thought patterns we currently use to support the structure of our lives, because we maintain many of the thought and life structures we live within subconsciously.

The following deep-thinking exercise will help you uncover the deeper structures in your life.

The Five Whys

The Five Whys is a simple but powerful exercise for uncovering the "root cause" behind just about anything. In terms of organizational development, the "root cause" refers to the cause of a problem at its deepest level. The best way to explain how a root cause analysis works is this example

(Figure 2.2) attributed to Don Messersmith a University of Maryland professor whose 1993 unpublished report for the National Park Service included a quintessential case study on the use of the Five Whys.

To help you understand the deeper motivations behind your vision, we will use a variation of the "Five Whys" process. By questioning your reasons for wanting what you want, you will reach a subconscious level of self-understanding about *why* you want what you want.

Look back at the *Rough Draft Vision #1* exercise you completed previously and saved to refer to later as needed. Ask yourself *why* you want the things stated in your rough draft vision.

If you had all the ultimate life reality you described in the rough draft of your vision, what would you have?

Problem: The Washington Monument Is Disintegrating

Q: *Why is the monument disintegrating?*
A: *Because of the use of harsh chemicals.*

Q: *Why do they need to use harsh chemicals?*
A: *To sufficiently clean pigeon poop off the monument.*

Q: *Why are there so many pigeons around the monument?*
A: *Because they eat spiders, and there are a lot of spiders around the monument.*

Q: *Why are there so many spiders?*
A: *Because they eat gnats, and there are a lot of gnats around the monument.*

Q: *Why are there so many gnats?*
A: *Because they are attracted to the monument's lights that come on at dusk.*

Final Solution: Turn on the lights of the monument at a later time. This will attract fewer gnats that in turn means fewer spiders and pigeons. Fewer pigeons result in less pigeon poop on the monument meaning less harsh chemicals are needed to clean it. This ultimately addresses the original problem of the disintegration of the Washington Monument.

Figure 2.2 Example of the Five Whys

WRITE IT DOWN

If you have just described material things such as a sports car, a bigger house, an art collection, and so on, ask yourself why you want those things. What would owning those material possessions give you? Be honest. Write down your answer.

WRITE IT DOWN

If you described more intangible rewards, like money to put your kids through school or purchasing a house for your mother, the question remains the same—why do you want those things? What would you have if you had well-educated children or a contented mother? Look for your deep motivation. The values you honor.

WRITE IT DOWN

Note: It is vital that you do not judge your answers! And I really do mean exactly that! Do not block your vision with negative thinking or judgment. There truly are no right or wrong answers for this exercise. You do not need to be better ... more worthy or nobler than you already are. If we are all part of a wider plan, wanting what you truly want is part of that plan. If you honestly want it enough to work hard to create it, it is good, worthy and noble.

Now ... keep going and ask yourself the same question at least two more times, "If I had this, what would I have?" For each answer you come up with, ask yourself the same question again, "Why do I want it?"

Once you have spent a sufficient amount of time thinking deeply about the roots of your desires, rewrite your rough draft of your vision.

For step-by-step instructions, see the vision statement worksheet in the workbook a the end of this chapter.

Draft Vision #2

WRITE IT DOWN

| |
| |
| |
| |

Has your vision changed?

Do Not Wait to Find Your Purpose

In Samuel Beckett's 1953 play, *Waiting for Godot*, two men wait endlessly and ultimately in vain for a man named Godot who never comes. If you are tempted to find your true (or divine) purpose in life simply through your vision for your business ... do not! Waiting for a purpose outside of yourself is like waiting for Godot.

Whatever you can imagine and are willing to work hard to create is your purpose. By creating a product that solves a problem for your market, you are fulfilling a purpose. If there is a market waiting for your solution, you and your business will be in service to something greater than yourself.

Do not get caught up in seeking a purpose with spiritual meaning or one of great passion. Like an arranged marriage, you will be most successful when you choose a business that meets what you both need and want in terms of income, lifestyle, and personal growth potential. You will find purpose as you bring your passion to the work of creating your ideal business.

Current Reality

Before we move on to the process of bringing your vision into actual existence, we need to define your current reality.

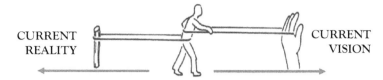

Figure 2.3 Robert Frtiz, creative tension

Your current reality is everything that is true about your life right now. Do not shy away from honestly assessing the gap between your current reality and the vision you plan to construct. You *want* to create tension. You will use this tension to motivate yourself. You will find this tension in the gap between what is true for you right now, on one hand, and your exciting vision of your future, on the other. Look again at Robert Fritz's illustration of creative tension. (Figure 2.3)

As you examine your current reality, you may find a gap between where you are and where you want to be. The gap may be in your current level of skills and/or the time you have available to build a new reality. Most often, the gap is about money; not having enough of it to use for building a better life.

We will be looking at the current reality of both your skill set and your available time, but let's start with money. To know your current financial reality you must thoughtfully consider what is true for you right now. Knowing your current money reality is important for creating the future of your dreams.

There are additional tools available in the workbook that will help you define and articulate your values and your vision as well as your finances. I highly recommend you spend a significant amount of time with the tools in the workbook in order to perform an honest assessment, both of your dream and your current reality. Remember, whatever reality is for you right now, it is neither good nor bad ... it just is. In addition, if it is not serving you and your vision well, it can be changed.

Highly Recommended

There are many useful tools available in the workbook that can help you get through the thinking process in the most productive ways. One of the most practical and most important tools provided in the workbook is the

Current Reality Analysis. By helping you gather and analyze your personal financial situation, including your personal income, expenses, liabilities, and assets, the *Current Reality Analysis* tool will help you navigate many of the decision points you will encounter while traveling this road to business success and a meaningful life.

Next Steps

In the next chapter, we will move beyond your personal vision, further developing your understanding of your current reality including your skills, talents, and abilities. Once you understand all that you bring to the table as a business leader, you can begin to develop an understanding of your mission. Once you appreciate *who* you can best serve and *how* you can serve them, you will be in a position to choose wisely from among your many brilliant business ideas.

Discovering your motivating and practical business mission is the next step in figuring things out on your path toward developing a customized business plan for yourself.

Module 2 Workbook—Getting Started: Envision What You Want

Learning Objectives

- Use a deep questioning technique to gain self-understanding.
- Describe the life you want for yourself.
- Identify your important personal and business values.
- Establish your current financial reality.

This is a self-coaching guide and, as such, it is about increasing your self-understanding. The visioning exercises in this module are intended to help you gain clarity about your own desire for a meaningful life. The value exercises will remind you about what you hold sacred in your life.

Finally, the *Current Reality Analysis* exercise will document your actual financial position. When, through deep thinking and writing, you have integrated these three different levels of self-understanding, you will be in a position to know:

- What you want?
- Why you want it?
- What you need to do to get it?

In this module you will find these exercises:

Visioning	Simple Vision Exercise
Information	What Are Values?
Thinking	Know Your Values
Self-Awareness	Five Simple Questions
Information	Your Current Reality
Knowledge	Reality and Money
Business Tool	Current Reality Analysis Tool

Index to Exercises

First Draft Visioning Exercise

What Is Your Vision?

Ask yourself: If I could be, do, or have anything, if time and money were no object, what would it be?

Be expansive. Be unrealistic. Be true to yourself. Write your answer down on paper. You will want to revisit your thinking as you continue with this book.

Note: It will not serve you to mark this unit as complete if you have not done the thinking exercise. Do it now before moving on.

What Are Values?

Values are beliefs and attitudes about the way things should be. Groups, societies, and cultures all have values that are shared by their members.

Why Do Your Values Matter?

When seeking to build a business to support your life in a way that has meaning for you, your values will guide you in your decisions about how you and your business appear in the world and how you spend your time.

Having a solid understanding of your values will help you maintain consistency in your decision making. When you know your deeply held values, you will know what is truly important for you in life.

The Thing About Values

All values are good values. Often good people are forced to choose between two good values:

- Adventure or Dependability
- Victory or Compassion
- Loyalty or Truth
- Honesty or Ambition

Because all values are good values, all values are relative. In order to choose the values most important to you, you will have to compare one to another and make a choice—a highly personal and sometimes difficult choice.

Beware: Values can be elusive. There is a tendency to "vote" for the most socially acceptable value over isolating those values you actually live out in action every day. Knowing your personal, deeply held values, may take some time, even months.

The next exercise will provide a starting point for your personal exploration of your values. Begin now, but plan to continue your explorations for months, even years to come.

Know Your Values

A Step-by-Step Method to Discover Your Own Values

To get you started, I have provided a list of common values (Figure 2.4). This list is in no way complete. You may have your own value words, or you may honor values not included on this list. Feel free to make this exercise your own. You can also find a pdf version of this *List of Values* on my website.

Directions

Step 1: From the list, choose 10 values that resonate with you. You may add others if you wish.

Step 2: Narrow your list of 10 values to a list of just three values.

Step 3: Keep the ones you cannot live without and toss the others out.

Step 4: Write down your top three values. You will want to refer back to this information as you create your vision for your life and your future.

Figure 2.4 List of common values

Five Simple Questions About Your Personal Vision

Vision without action is a dream. Action without vision is simply passing the time. Action with vision is making a positive difference.

—Joel Barke

The process of clarifying your deeper motivations for your vision, including establishing the details of what you want and why you want it, and firmly establishing your intentions by writing it down, is by far the hardest part of self-awareness and, ultimately, of business leadership. It is also the most important, so do not shirk the hard work of thinking.

But First... Begin at the Beginning

What do you want? And, more importantly, why do you want it?

The rule here is: it must be expressed in the positive not the negative. Do not say. "I want a business that will let me quit my job," instead say, "I want to build a business that will make a steady profit of (name your number)."

How to Manifest Your Vision

Say out loud and in specific detail what it is you want for your life. You may want a big business of your own or you may want a surf shop on a beach in Spain. You may want a loving relationship or you may want to travel the world. Whatever it is you want, be *very* specific about what it is. Describe the color, the taste, and the smell. What you can see and hear? Who shares this vision with you? When you have described in detail what you want to create in your life, then ask yourself: Why? Why do you want to have whatever it is you have described? If you had the vision you can imagine, what would that get you?

Continue with the following exercise to drill down till you have uncovered your core values.

Decide What You Want

Having trouble deciding on a vision for your life? If you are not sure, try this:

- Make up a vision. Be spontaneous.
- Borrow one that sounds good.
- Use this Personal Vision Worksheet to deepen your thinking. To download a copy visit the website https://www.small-businessleadershipnow.com/units/five-shockingly-simple-questions-clarify-vision/

Personal Vision Worksheet

No problem can withstand the assault of sustained thinking.

—Voltaire

Thinking Exercise

- What are the 10 things you most enjoy doing? Be honest. These are the 10 things without which your weeks, months, and years would feel incomplete.
- What three things must you do every single day to feel fulfilled in your life?
- If you never had to work another day in your life, how would you spend your time instead of working?
- When your life is ending, what will you regret not doing, seeing, or achieving?

Writing

In five years I am _____ years old

In five years I feel _____

In five years I am _____

In five years I contribute by _____

In five years my achievements include _____

In five years I've experienced _____

In five years I love _____

In five years I'm surrounded by _____

In five years I'm a point of inspiration and influence for _____

In five years I'm helping to being into the world _____

Exercise: The Five Whys

Now for the Good Part

Pick a vision, any vision. The first version of your vision is not all that important because we are going to deconstruct it until the truth lies revealed like a precious piece of beach glass.

Step One: The First Why

Why do you want this vision? Or, to put it another way, if you had it, what would it get you? For example, one of my clients, Rachel, envisions a business that will produce the same or more income than she is currently making by providing her career counseling services online. Her "whys?" include:

- To gain more free time by eliminating office hours
- To capture her career counseling knowledge and experience
- To allow her to work from home, wherever that home may be

Steps Two, Three, and Four: More Whys

Take each of your answers and ask "why?" about each one. The expected outcome here is to trace your vision back to its source.

Why #2: What Would Why #1 Get You?

As Rachel examines her vision, she realizes she wants to be free to purchase property on a lake outside of town.

Why #3: And What Would That Get You?

Rachel's answer: a sense of accomplishment and independence.

The Back Story

What this answer revealed to Rachel was the backstory that was, unconsciously, influencing her choices. The house on the lake was a vision shared with her former fiancé. When the relationship failed, Rachel lost not only her connection to her vision, but she also encountered financial challenges that caused her to work more hours than she wanted.

Why #4: What Would That Get You?

Rachel realized that buying the lake property would signal that she was no longer injured by the demise of her relationship. That sense of accomplishment and independence was the thing she needed to move on and build a new life without her former lover.

Why #5: What Would That Bring You?

Rachel's answer: happiness. By articulating the root cause of her business vision, Rachel was able to recognize that the lake property, and the self-generated money to purchase it, was not the final goal of her vision. Her core value, the real vision, was a sense of satisfaction and happiness with her life *as it is.* Knowing this, she can choose many possible paths to a sense of accomplishment and independence.

Self-Realization Rocks

Like Rachel, you too are motivated by forces and perceptions you may not fully recognize. If your intention is to build a business that satisfies your soul, self-knowledge is freedom. As you work through this exercise with each of your life or business goals, you will probably find you keep coming back to the same few primary goals. These few goals should reflect your core values. When you can wake each day to a task list that promotes these values, your life will have meaning and joy. Moreover, when your business promotes these values to others, it will be profitable.

Your Current Reality

In order to create the tension that is a fundamental part of the creative process, you will need to acknowledge your current reality.

Current Reality and You

Your understanding of your reality should be real, not pessimistic and not overly optimistic. When it comes to working with the tension between your current reality and your vision, the key to sustained success is balance.

The Stockdale Paradox

Jim Stockdale was a United States military officer during the Vietnam War. When his plane was shot down, he was held captive for eight years, tortured and denied medical attention. Despite his overwhelming reasons to despair, Stockdale became a leader of the captive's resistance movement.

After his release in 1973, Stockdale was interviewed for a business book by author James C. Collins, *Good to Great: Why Some Companies Make the Leap—And Others Do Not.* In this classic business volume, Collins writes about a conversation he had with Stockdale regarding his coping strategy during his period in the Vietnamese POW camp:

I never lost faith in the end of the story, I never doubted not only that I would get out, but also that I would prevail in the end and turn the experience into the defining event of my life, which, in retrospect, I would not trade.

When Collins asked who did not make it out of Vietnam, Stockdale replied:

Oh, that's easy, the optimist. Oh, they were the ones who said, 'We are going to be out of here by Christmas.' And Christmas would come, and Christmas would go. Then they'd say, 'We're going to be out by Easter.' And Easter would come, and Easter would go. And then Thanksgiving, and then it would be Christmas again. And they died of a broken heart.

Stockdale then added:

This is a very important lesson. You must never confuse faith that you will prevail in the end—which you can never afford to lose—with the discipline to confront the most brutal facts of your current reality, whatever they might be.

Hopefully, the facts of your current reality are not brutal.

Your Current Reality

Your *Current Reality* includes not only the forces working against your success but also your freely adopted priorities and the responsibilities that go with them; your preferred lifestyle and maintenance costs associated with your choices and, of course, your financial resources—or lack thereof.

Once you know what you want, it is wise to take stock of the resources you already have on hand to help you create your vision as well as potential challenges you will need to address.

In later lessons, we will inventory the skills and abilities you have to help you along the way. Right now, we are going to take a look at the elephant in the room: your personal financial reality.

Remember, your current reality is just your current reality. You can change it.

Money and Your Current Reality

Okay, so far, our exploration of your reality has been subjective and, frankly, a little on the fluffy side. Now is it time to put on your hard-nosed business leader's hat and get real about your numbers.

Sad but True

It takes money to make money. There is no way to get around the hard, cold reality of survival. You *need* to have money. You may not need as much as you think, or you may need much, much more than you think. It is time, right now, to find out.

Your Current Reality Analysis

This next tool, the *Current Reality Analysis,* is a study in the current reality of all your income and expenses. If you want to begin thinking like a business owner and entrepreneur, completing this worksheet is mandatory. There is no wiggle room. You must know your numbers.

Resistance Is Futile

This exercise is by far the most emotional part of this business building process. If you do not know how much you have, how much you need, and how much you eventually want, this exercise will help you find out.

I have a client who, based on his observations of the meager retirement faced by both his grandmother and father, decided he needed to put 20 percent of his income away in long-term savings. The challenge for him was, based on his current income and family obligations, that this number represented serious hardships for himself and his family.

When I questioned him about the reality behind the numbers, it became clear his 20 percent figure was a fear-based reaction. He did not *know* what 20 percent savings would provide for him over the intervening 25 years until his retirement. Nor did he know what a more comfortable saving plan, say 10 percent, might provide for him at retirement.

Despite the fact his children were still very young, he was eager for his wife to return to work and reluctant to consider superior but expensive private education for his children. He was making these very real and painful sacrifices in order to meet an arbitrary target of 20 percent.

This vague but distressing fear of not having enough money is like fearing the boogeyman. I am *very* familiar with this monster. I spent years of my life, working at corporate jobs that made me unhappy because I was afraid, in some vague way, that I would not have enough money. Or, more accurately, afraid that I would be needy and dependent on others because I did not have money.

The *Current Reality Analysis* is a tool designed to help you KNOW the truth of your money situation. Once you know it, you can make a plan to address the reality, build creative tension, and start work to create a new reality around money.

Do Not Give In to the Boogeyman

If you find yourself resisting the completion of this exercise, explore your relationship to money and your choice about how you spend it. If you feel shame, it may be because you are acting against your values. Alternatively, it may be because you are acting against someone else's values. Figure it out. When you do, you will feel much better.

Just Do It

Follow the instructions in the next lesson and do not procrastinate. Knowing your current reality is both necessary and freeing.

Know Your Financial Reality

In order to know what you need to do to create your personal vision, you will need to know what is currently true about your finances, including what comes in and what goes out every month.

To know—really know—you will need data. For data, you will need your bank, credit card, and loan statements.

But wait: Before you run off to gather up all your unopened mail, take some time to review this tool and the *accompanying instructional video*. Take time to think realistically about your personal sources of income and your personal expenses. Listen closely to your internal dialogue. What are you telling yourself about your current financial situation? Is your self-talk positive or negative? *How do you know what you believe about your money is true?*

When you have entered the true numbers for *all* your income and expenses, you will know your current financial reality. When your reality is displayed before you in actual data, ask yourself:

How does my reality compare to what I thought I knew before I began this exercise?

Following (Figure 2.5) is a simple tool to help you record the numbers of your Current Financial Reality.

You can access a working copy of this spreadsheet https://smallbusinessleadershipnow.com/wp-content/uploads/2014/05/Current-Reality-Excel-Spreadsheet.xlsx and detailed instructions for completing this analysis on my website: *Current Reality Analysis Tool (Video and Download)* https://smallbusinessleadershipnow.com/units/current-reality-analysis-downloads/ *Note: You do not need to use an Excel spreadsheet provided on the website. When you recreate this simple spreadsheet using paper and a calculator it will be enough.*

Current Reality

Client Name _____   Date _____

Where are you now?   Net Worth | $ - |

Income

Source	Amount
TOTAL	$ -

Assets

Source	Amount
TOTAL	$ -

Expenses

Source	Amount
TOTAL	$ -

Liabilities

Source	Amount
TOTAL	$ -

Figure 2.5 Simple current reality spreadsheet

CHAPTER 3

Vision Versus Current Reality: Which Business Is Right for You?

To see things differently than other people, the most effective solution is to bombard the brain with things it has never encountered before.
—Gregory Berns

Now that you have created the initial draft of your personal vision and you have an awareness of the solid ground that makes up the configuration of your current reality, you are ready to figure out what type of business will be the foundation of your future. Think of your business as the *system* that is going to support the structure of your life in a way that will honor you: your values, your priorities, your unique skills, and your talents.

Do Not Let Decisions Freak You Out!

Entrepreneurs, in general, are a creative bunch. You probably have many … dozens … perhaps even hundreds of interesting business ideas. Yet even when you are quite clear about what is important to you, choosing between multiple brilliant ideas can be difficult. You may feel like your ideas are all so brilliant it will be impossible to choose just one. Fear of missing a better opportunity can cause debilitating indecision. Indecision can be destructive to your success.

Relax! This is not a marriage. When you choose one idea with strong potential, you are laying the foundation for many possible businesses to come. Get this one right and the next one will be easier. And the good news is … again … this is not a marriage! Unlike being bound to a spouse, you do not have to give up one business in order to start another one. You can have as many active businesses as you want.

You truly can have it all, and in the case of business ownership, you can have it all at the same time as long as you structure each business in ways to make this possible.

Multiple Sources of Income

If you are currently working a J.O.B. and simultaneously starting a business, you already understand the advantages of multiple sources of income.

For example, my young and talented massage therapist works as an *au pair* in the mornings because her massage business is not yet thriving to the point of having enough customers to keep her busy all day.

Another client of mine starts his workday very early so he can switch his focus to his other business late in the afternoon without negatively impacting his primary job. Mornings are for his "day job" while afternoons are when he coaches other people with similar technical strengths about how to reach their powerful professional and business goals.

The same piece-meal building process with a steady focus on your goals, combined with hard work and consistent action, can eventually build significant income. The financial increase from your entrepreneurial enterprises will ultimately replace your regular J.O.B. When I was in this transitional process myself, I actually had three businesses up and running at one point.

It is important that you do not allow the fear of having to let go of something stop you from doing all you can to reach your ultimate goals. In this chapter, you will uncover the current reality of your own personal talents and abilities along with the skills, knowledge, and experience you have acquired over your lifetime thus far. When you truly realize all of the skills and gifts you possess, you will be able to use this self-understanding to develop a clear vision of a business that will provide the income you need along with joy and contentment at the same time.

Once you know what personal characteristics, skills, attitudes, experiences, and knowledge you bring to the table, you can then utilize the powerful creativity and analysis tools provided to invite insight and inspiration into your life. While still living within your current reality, you will be able to identify an inspired business model that will eventually generate the money you need to support the fabulous life you have envisioned.

Of Course, You Have Skills, but You Also Have Knowledge and Experience

Some people want to start a business because they are passionate about something like art, green energy, health, and so on. Other people have a tendency to wander from the straight path of their career in order to smell the flowers along the way. They embody the process of becoming the proverbial jack-of-all-trades but the master of none.

Whatever path you have followed, you have acquired significant skills, experience, and knowledge along the way. You do not have to be a *master* of whatever business niche you choose, but you do need to have a working knowledge of it. Your role is to be a business builder, not a technical expert in the area you choose. In order to build your business, you only need to know more about your product than the people you serve. If a high level of expertise is necessary, you can always hire an expert or subcontract for that portion of your business.

People tell me, "I have no skills," all the time, but I never believe it. The trick is to stop comparing yourself to people who have more than you, whether it is more knowledge, more experience, or more nerve. If you must compare yourself to anyone, compare yourself with people who have *less* of those attributes than you do.

One of my clients came to me with a perceived self-image of having "no skills." However, as we talked, I discovered she had a working knowledge of Reiki healing along with a deep love for her eight cats. You may be thinking there was not much she could do with those seemingly insignificant skills and characteristics, but she created a successful business centered around providing Reiki for cats. That might seem like a small, unimportant niche in the business world, but when she added products like organic cat food and specialized supplements to her business, she tapped into a fairly unknown market niche of providing services for health-conscious cat lovers. Of course, there were many people who knew more about Reiki than my client did, and many others who knew more about cats than she did, but she had a unique skill set combination and was able to slide right into the available spot in a unique market niche.

William Bridges is an author and consultant who advises both individuals and organizations going through a transition. He has written very helpful books and sold over a million copies. When recalling the early days of his business, Bridges writes, "I provided the expertise (which consisted largely of being a page or two ahead of the group in the understanding of transition), but I learned as much from them as they did from me."

It's time to be bold! Begin the assessment of your skills and knowledge by listing your particular interests and skills. Do not be shy or humble at this point. Make sure you acknowledge all the benefits you bring to the table. The exercises here and the deeper exploration in the workbook exercises can help get you started.

Remember, you want to compare yourself and your skills, knowledge, experience and attitudes against people who have less of these characteristics than you do in any given area of interest. How can you help these people?

Skills Inventory

Your personal skills, knowledge, and abilities are your particular gifts. Your potential to contribute value to the world is an extension of these gifts. Take the time to acknowledge everything you have to offer. Begin by remembering your past experiences, both good and bad, and probe each experience to uncover the skills you used to maneuver through the various circumstances.

WRITE IT DOWN

| |
| |
| |
| |

List Your Experiences—Make sure to include paid jobs, volunteer roles, leadership positions, internships, academic projects, professional development, and any other additional training, hobbies, interests, and areas of knowledge.

Think about each experience—imagine you are writing your autobiography for future generations and seek to portray yourself truthfully and in the best possible light. After all, you want your descendants to be proud of where they came from. Tell the story of your life experience honestly, but use your skills and talents as the focal point.

Here (Figure 3.1) are some specific skills you may recognize in yourself:

Leadership	Motivation	Communications
Listening	Personal relations	Negotiations
Ethics	Creative thinking	Planning and organizing
Decision making	Business knowledge	Industry specific knowledge
Financial knowledge	Opportunity recognition	Technical knowledge

Figure 3.1 Acknowledge your skills

What Else Do You Have?

In addition to skills and knowledge acquired over a lifetime, you also have unique personal qualities or an inherent character. If you have undergone character education in school, you may recognize such qualities as responsibility, kindness, honesty, fairness, teamwork, persistence, and courage as some of the more positive aspects of one's character.

Since the beginning of this century, character has gained recognition in those scientific communities that study the psychology of happiness. Numerous studies have found that each human being has a distinct collection of character strengths and each person uses their inherent strengths in different ways depending on the situation.

The science of positive psychology has shown that when you use your character strengths to navigate the circumstances of your life, you will increase your general happiness. It is wise then to consider your personal strengths and virtues when designing the business you will create.

There are 24 universally recognized character strengths. For more information and an assessment to help you identify your particular strengths, see the materials online.

What Else?

When you begin to acknowledge your skills, knowledge, abilities, values, and character strengths, you can begin to see that there is something, a product or a service, you are uniquely prepared to offer to the world.

It is important for you and for the people you can serve to recognize and claim all the power you have. Do not let negative self-talk discourage you from claiming your power. Write down your personal insights. Capture your strengths on paper; you will use this information about yourself to explore those markets that you are best able to serve.

If, despite my encouragement, you are still thinking, "I do not have any real talents," you will find information about various assessment tools at the end of this chapter. These scientific assessments are impartial evaluations that can reveal truths about your gifts. Truths you may be unwilling to acknowledge. If your negative self-talk is holding you back, you can trust the impartial scientific community to identify the innate strengths and the aptitudes that you bring to any situation.

Once you clearly understand what you are good at, what you are interested in, what is important to you, and what you know how to *do*, it is then time to see how you can use your skills, knowledge, experiences, and abilities to help someone else, somewhere in the world.

What Are Your Priorities?

I hope that you will take some time to access the information in the workbook and to explore your personal gifts. I hope you will be excited about the discoveries you make. Before we move on to using your insights to reveal your mission, let us create some motivating tension by assessing your current reality.

It is true that you have skills, talents, knowledge, and abilities. You also have a life and your life includes your priorities and responsibilities. Your roles, responsibilities and the values you hold dear determine your priorities. In his book, *First Things First*, the late Stephen Covey relates the following story:

One day, an expert was speaking to a group of business students and, to drive home a point, used an illustration…

As this man stood in front of the group of high-powered overachievers he said, "Okay, time for a quiz." Then he pulled out a one-gallon, wide-mouthed mason jar and set it on a table in front of him. Then he produced about a dozen fist-sized rocks and carefully placed them, one at a time, into the jar.

When the jar was filled to the top and no more rocks would fit inside, he asked, "Is this jar full?" Everyone in the class said, "Yes." Then he said, "Really?" He reached under the table and pulled out a bucket of gravel. Then he dumped some gravel in and shook the jar causing pieces of gravel to work themselves down into the spaces between the big rocks.

Then he smiled and asked the group once more, "Is the jar full?" By this time the class was onto him. "Probably not," one of them answered. "Good!" he replied. And he reached under the table and brought out a bucket of sand. He started dumping the sand in and it went into all the spaces left between the rocks and the gravel. Once more he asked the question, "Is this jar full?"

"No!" the class shouted. Once again he said, "Good!" Then he grabbed a pitcher of water and began to pour it in until the jar was filled to the brim. Then he looked up at the class and asked, "What is the point of this illustration?"

One eager beaver raised his hand and said, "The point is, no matter how full your schedule is, if you try really hard, you can always fit some more things into it!"

"No," the speaker replied, "that's not the point. The truth this illustration teaches us is: If you do not put the big rocks in first, you'll never get them in at all."

What are the big rocks in *your* life? A project you want to accomplish? More time with your loved ones? Your faith? Education? Finances? A cause you are passionate about? Teaching or mentoring others?

Your priorities and values will determine what your big rocks are. Remember to put the biggest rocks in first or you will never get them in at all. Creating a vision for your business that *doesn't* allow time for your biggest rocks will ultimately lead to frustration and stress. Establish your big rocks now.

Life Priorities

What are your life priorities? The structure or configuration of your life includes a combination of many roles: parent, citizen, leader, boss, friend, learner, homeowner, spouse, sibling, employee, church leader, friend, teacher, community member, child, and so on. Of course, these are just examples of the many functions a person may fulfill, so in the following exercise (Figure 3.2) make sure to list all of the roles that are personally meaningful to you.

Your Ranking	Example
1.	Spouse
2.	Parent
3.	Child
4.	Sibling
5.	Employer
6.	Friend
7.	Business Partner
8.	Mentor
9.	Leader
10.	Learner

Figure 3.2 Acknowledge your priorities

You will also need to rank your priorities in whatever order of importance they are in your life by first ranking the most important functions followed by the ones that are not as much of a priority to you. Rank them by whatever factors seem relevant in *your* own life such as the time required, level of passion, and importance to your lifestyle, and so on.

Exercise: My Life Priorities

Use this exercise to determine your most important priorities in the following categories:

- Family Member
- Friend
- Relations with Significant Others and Romance
- Fun and Recreation
- Health
- Money
- Personal Growth
- Physical Environment
- Career

For each area of your life, visualize what the best possible outcome would be for that particular role. How will your business support you in achieving your dream outcomes?

Be sure to explore the exercises in the workbook to continue to assess your own personal strengths and talents.

Find Your Niche and Identify Your First Target Market

Similar to choosing one business idea, choosing one appropriate niche can also be frightening. It can feel like a loss of possibilities but remember … this is just your *first* business. When you are ready to do more, you can always expand. In the meantime, you will find it infinitely easier and more rewarding to work with a demographic group that responds enthusiastically to who you are, what you know, and what you can offer.

Be careful not to be caught up in advanced market analysis. Even Facebook Founder Mark Zuckerberg started simply with just Harvard students who needed a way to communicate.

Who Do You Know?

Who do you know? Who are your friends? Relatives? Acquaintances? Who is in your sphere of influence? Take a moment to write down the names of 100 people you know.

Then ask yourself, what problems do these people have that you could help solve with a product or a service?

For more detailed instructions, see the exercise in the workbook at the end of this chapter.

When you have listed 100 people and you have given some deep thought to the problems they are dealing with, you have laid the groundwork for the next exercise. The next exercise is a creative act of brainstorming to discover your unique market and the particular product or service you are uniquely qualified to provide to the market.

How to Mindfully Discover Your Perfect Business

Finding a market—a unique group of people with a specific set of problems you are uniquely qualified to solve—is the key to success for any small business. Even though it is so important, many business owners I coach struggle to define their niche in the market and what value their business can offer to that niche. Through the years, I have discovered the intense process of clearly focusing their motivation to serve and add value to the world, in some way or another, is one of the hardest parts of the business creation process.

The world as we have created it is a process of our thinking. It cannot be changed without changing our thinking.

—Albert Einstein

We Are All Creative

The secret of your potential business lies hidden in your unconscious mind. The key to discovering the market you can best serve lies in your ability to change your thinking patterns in order to tap into your hidden creativity.

The good news is the fact that we are all creative and resourceful. We are all capable of finding a unique and inspiring answer to the important question, "What business are you in?"

The mind of man is capable of anything—because everything is in it, all the past as well as the future.

—Joseph Conrad, Heart of Darkness

How to Use Your Mind

You may believe that your mind and your brain are the same thing, and perhaps you have "racked your brain" to come up with an answer to the question of "What business are you in?" If so, stop and reconsider now. The answer isn't in your brain. The answer is in your mind.

Your brain is a physical organ while your mind is consciousness plus something else. Your mind may be a window to your soul, a link to the shared universe, or even a vibration, and so on. I have my ideas on the topic, and I will allow you to have yours because the proverbial mind versus body debate is interesting but far beyond the scope of this book. However, I do want to encourage you to use the inherent abilities of your brain to uncover the secrets held in your mind.

How to Use the Your Brain to Create Insight

Following are six hidden "behaviors" of the brain. When you are mindful or consciously aware of these hidden behaviors, you will be better able to create "Ah, ha!" moments on demand. Each of these previously unknown brain reactions has the ability to access that larger and more mysterious entity—your mind. It is in the deeper regions of your mind that the answers to your questions about your business reside.

As you learn about these hidden behaviors of your brain, observe your own brain. Watch for these hidden brain behaviors as you prepare your mind for a successful brainstorming session.

> *Think left and think right and think low and think high. Oh, the*
> *thinks you can think up if only you try!*
>
> —Dr. Seuss

The Secrets to Creating Inspiration on Demand

Have a Broad Mindset

I have worked with many people in an effort to uncover their unique business ideas. When they are asked to probe their interests for market ideas, I hear things like vegetarians, single parents, doll collectors, or ham radio operators—just to name a few. While these may all be good ideas of themselves, because of the way your brain seeks patterns and certainty, initial ideas can often create a block to recognizing additional creative insights.

For now, I want you to jot down your first thoughts about who you serve and how you serve them. If you completed the previous exercises, you should have a list of 100 people you know and the problems they face. Go back to the list and think about how you could solve one of their problems. How could you meet a need? Write down whatever comes to mind and use those thoughts to broaden your mindset in order to think of even more problems that you might be able to help with.

To find your perfect market niche, you need to think in wider circles than those provided by your initial thoughts on the matter. Look at the list you created and ask yourself, "What else?" For example, perhaps you listed the mothers of your child's preschool friends as people you know.

Ask yourself, "What can I do to help them? Who else do I know from the pre-school? Who else knows me?" What do they need or want? If you were to meet and get to know more people from that environment, who might they be? Expand your mindset to include people you might get to know in the future. You will be able to form a new idea better when you combine distantly related information.

To expand your creative processes even further, there are additional tools available at the end of this chapter, including a classic brainstorming technique from a book on creative thinking entitled *Six Thinking Hats, by Edward de Bono.*

Let It Go

While it is helpful to be an expert in your field, set that aside for a moment and allow the universe to speak to you. In other words, do not be *too* smart! You are an expert in your field because your brain has already mapped certain processes in that field to the point where you can complete these processes easily without conscious attention. You are skilled in your field because you can perform the majority of your responsibilities effortlessly.

Turning new experiences into repeatable routines is what our brains do for us. When any skill is new, it takes conscious thought to perform. But as we gain competence through experience, we no longer have to think so much about our performance. The ability of our brain to develop unconscious competence is the very thing that allows us to operate a motor vehicle, for example. Driving is a complex process, but our brain allows us to learn how to drive so skillfully that we no longer have to think about it while we are doing it. This leaves our minds free to plan dinner on our way home instead of having to focus solely on driving.

However, the problem is when your brain takes you down these familiar and subconscious pathways, it also returns to the same old pattern of thinking. In order to gain new insight, you need to use the existing maps in your brain in new ways.

If you think you know who loved your particular problem solution in the past (i.e., preschool moms, vegetarians, single parents, doll collectors, ham radio operators, etc.), you will be well served if you stop your mind from traveling down that same path. As Edward De Bono says, "You cannot dig a hole in a new place by digging the same hole deeper."

However, to stop your thoughts from traveling the same familiar path, you need to be mindful. You need to notice when you are stuck in the same thinking patterns so you can make a conscious decision to stop the pattern and "dig" in a different place.

Close the Door

Literally, close the door, shut down the computer, and silence the phone. If you have ever tried to meditate, you know how quickly your mind will leap to follow the least distraction. To discover the creative idea that is waiting for you, you will need to tune into quiet, subtle nudges, whispery thoughts, and intuitions. To hear the universe speaking, you will need to be quiet, so close the door.

Do Not Worry—Be Happy

Your emotional state is an important component of your ability to tune into your creative ideas. When you are anxious, there is too much "noise" (real electrical activity in your brain) for you to hear the whispers of your destiny.

A 55-year-old client of mine feared that she was too old to start a new business. Her question was not, "Who can I serve?" Instead, she asked me, "Am I crazy?" Clearly, her anxiety about her age needed to be resolved before she could tune into her true calling.

So ... what are *your* thoughts at this point? Identify any self-limiting beliefs you may have and make a conscious choice to silence them for the duration of this exercise. After all, you can always pick them up again when you are done here—or not.

For more information about recognizing your unconscious beliefs and silencing the ones that are self-limiting, view the workbook at the end of this chapter.

Go Out and Play

If you have been following along so far, and you've been taking notes and checking off each idea as you actively seek a new and innovative business idea for yourself, stop for a bit now and take a break—have some fun, laugh a bit, win a hand of solitaire, and so on. If you take some time to do whatever defines "fun" in your life, you will discover that you have better ideas afterward. Go ahead ... take a break. The universe and the target market for your business idea will wait...

On the other hand, if you *have not* done the work up to this point, but the excuse to quit and take a break resonates within, it is time to rethink your motivation. Ask yourself (and answer honestly!), "What is going on with me right now?"

Thinking is the hardest work there is, which is probably the reason why so few engage in it.

—Henry Ford

Be Kind to Your Mind

Finally, use your brain deliberately to harness the power of your mind. To do this, you first need to change your thinking by *thinking about your thinking*. A quiet and non-judgmental observation of the current reality of your thinking is similar to the spiritual concept of mindfulness. In a sense, you want to detach from your thinking in order to analyze it.

Ask yourself:

- How long have I been thinking about this market?
- How committed am I to pursuing this idea?
- What is the insight brewing deep within my mind?

These questions will help you to think consciously about your thinking. By stopping the default processes your brain automatically enacts, you will be better able to recognize when you are traveling familiar neural pathways. Thinking about your thinking will encourage deep insights to surface and be recognized.

David Rock, the founder of Results Coaching, has reduced the process of seeking insight to a four-phase model he calls ARIA—**A**wareness, **R**eflection, **I**nsight, and **A**ction.

Awareness

When you become aware of an impasse in your thinking, you need to relax and quit looking for more of the same. Be aware of your thinking and stop digging deeper and deeper along the same thought pathways. Try reducing your thinking efforts to simple terms such as considering "Who can I best serve?" instead of "Which vegetarians between the ages of 25 and 45 have I not yet approached?"

Reflection

Seek loose connections. Hold such an impasse lightly in your mind, but do not focus on it. Instead, pay attention to your thought pattern. Look for genius ideas thrown up from the right hemisphere of your brain. Relax and aim for a drowsy and unfocused mental state.

Insight

When insight comes, you will definitely know it because the moment of insight creates a specific energy response in your brain. When you have an insight, you will not only feel it, it will actually feel good.

Action

You know that insight you just discovered. *Write it down*!

Our brains automatically return to the default thought processes that run through our minds all the time: your shoes pinch, you forgot to charge your phone, or there is a parent-teacher conference tonight. The energetic "high" your insight produces will not last long, so be careful to capture the insight immediately or it will sink back down into the mysterious depths from whence it came.

> *Where your talents and the needs of the world cross, there lies your vocation.*
>
> —Aristotle

What to Do With Your Insight

Once you have gained insight about your unique business possibilities, take some time to allow the answers to the following simple questions to emerge:

- Whom do you serve?
- What problem do you solve for them?

The inspirational answer is already yours. You just need to gently manage the workings of your brain in order to further unleash the genius of your mind.

Take your time to get it right because once you have captured your inspiration, it will be time for the other 90 percent of the task—perspiration. With your insight carefully captured, it is now time for the hard work of getting clear about how your inspiration will manifest in the real world.

Develop a Mission Statement

In the next chapter, you will begin to develop your business plan. Before you begin, it is important to be very clear about the overall intent of your business idea. When you are able to describe the purpose of your business in just a few direct sentences (sentences that are clear and inspiring to others), you will have developed the mission statement for your business.

To express your insight in a mission statement, answer the following questions:

- Why are you in business?
- Who are your customers?
- What image do you want to convey with your business?
- What is the nature of your product or service?
- What is the underlying philosophy or the values of your business?

Next ... condense your thinking thus far in the process. Consider your thoughts about your business, your purpose, your market, and your product, and state your mission clearly to answer the question, "What are you trying to do?"

This exercise is for your clarity and inspiration. You will further refine your understanding as you continue to think deeply about your business. Consider this the first draft of your ideas. Use the following big business mission statements as examples only. Your business mission must reflect your unique value to the world.

Microsoft's mission is "a computer on every desk and in every home, all running Microsoft software." Amazon's mission statement for its Kindle reading device is "every book ever printed in any language, all available in less than 60 seconds."

What is *your* mission statement?

WRITE IT DOWN

For more resources to help you think deeper about your business mission, visit the workbook.

What If You Still Do Not Know?

You may have one clear idea about your mission, but you may still have a treasure chest of ideas on how to fulfill that mission. If so, now is the time to once again consider all your options and choose *one* idea to develop and define with your mission statement. Remember—this is not your final choice! This is just your *first* choice.

To select the best option out of all your brilliant ideas, answer the following questions about your vision, current reality, and value system:

- Does this business have the potential to support your vision?
- Do you have, or can you get, the time and money you need to start up your business idea?
- Will this business support your values and important life roles?
- Does it embrace your "big rocks"?

Before we finish this chapter, there are a few more important and practical questions you need to consider. While your business *is* your creative gift to the world, it is also your livelihood. Before you invest significant time and money in its creation, you need to make sure it will meet your income requirements.

Your Market Niche

Now that you have insight into who your business is meant to serve, you should have the information you need to get crystal clear on your market demographic. Your market is your market, but is it big enough to sustain your business? Answer these questions:

- How would you describe your ideal customer?
- Whom do you want to work with in terms of age, income, gender, likes, dislikes, hobbies, activities, and so on?
- Where will you find these people? Where do they spend their time? What do they read, watch, and talk about? What are the keywords for their lives?
- Whom do you already know who would be willing to help you?
- How many of those people would you like to have as your customers?

Who Will Pay?

It is a common mistake to focus on providing a service to the so-called "needy" or your friends and family without first considering how you will make a living with that service. Good intentions aside, selling a product to people who cannot afford to buy it is a losing game. You need to choose a market segment that wants *and can afford* your solution to their needs. Once your business is successful, you can contribute to the needy (or your friends and loved ones) through planned contributions, business sponsorships, on-the-job training, and so on.

Look back at the description you developed for your market niche. Can those people afford to pay for your product or service? *Will* they pay for it? If the answer is "no," go back to the previous exercise and seek another insightful idea. Moreover, do not worry … the universe is generous! All you have to do is listen.

Next Steps

In the next chapter, we will turn our attention to creating a specific business vision based on the mission of the business you plan to create. So far, we have used your own thinking, standard coaching techniques, and the power of your mind to set the groundwork for creating a business that honors your values and your unique skills as it supports and enhances your chosen life path. Now we shall shift the focus to the specifics of the business that will create the income you need for the life you have envisioned.

The thinking exercises you will now do in order to capture your goal-oriented business vision will take your aspiring business idea one-step closer to reality. Are you excited?

It is awfully important to know what is and what is not your business.
—Gertrude Stein

Module 3 Workbook: Vision Versus Current Reality: Which Business Is Right for You?

Learning Objectives

- Recognize and appreciate your innate skills, talents, abilities, and character strengths.
- Make connections between your personal vision, your business vision, and your current responsibilities and roles.
- Learn to use creative thinking tools to expand and deepen your understanding of your possibilities.
- Write a clear and inspiring mission statement for your business based on your self-understanding of your skills, strengths, values and current reality.

In what ways do your personal skills, talents, abilities, and inherent strengths contribute to your business? When you have explored and acknowledged all your natural gifts, you will be well equipped to seek an inspiring business idea.

The tools provided here will help you recognize all you bring to the table as a business leader. Once you have acknowledged and accepted your strengths, you will be in a position to:

- Brainstorm additional possibilities.
- Recognize any self-limiting beliefs that may be holding you back.
- Develop an inspiring mission for your business.

In the workbook, you will find the following tools to help you in your quest to find your perfect business:

Exercise	My Skills Inventory
Exercise	More Life Priorities
Exercise	How to Generate 100 Leads
Exercise	My Talents and Strengths
Tool	Tools for Brainstorming
Tool	How to Map Your Mind
Exercise	Self-Limiting Beliefs
Exercise	My Mission Statement

Index to Exercises

More Skills Inventory

Your innate and acquired skills, knowledge, and abilities are your gifts. Your potential to contribute to the world through your business is an extension of these gifts. Do not hide your gifts, use them!

Acknowledge Yourself

Take time to acknowledge to yourself all that you have to offer. Begin by brainstorming your past experience, both good and bad, and analyze each experience for the skills you used to maneuver the circumstances.

List Your Experiences

Include paid jobs, volunteer roles, leadership positions, internships, academic projects, professional development, additional training, hobbies, interests, and areas of knowledge.

Think

Imagine you are writing your autobiography for your descendants and seeking to portray yourself in the best possible light. After all, you want your family to be proud of where they came from. Now tell the story of that experience honestly but with your skills as the focal point.

Now list the skills you demonstrated in your story.

WRITE IT DOWN

More Life Priorities

What is it that makes your life worth living? Doing work you enjoy is important, of course, but your relationships are also important contributors to your happy life.

With each relationship in your life, you play a role. Take time now to inventory the roles you play. Recognize which roles bring you joy, which bring you a sense of fulfillment and satisfaction and which roles, perhaps inherited from others, might be better left alone.

What Are Your Life Roles?

You may be one or all of these: parent, citizen, leader, boss, friend, learner, householder, spouse, sibling, employee, church leader, friend, teacher, community member, child, and so on. Think of all the roles you play in your life.

WRITE IT DOWN

| |
| |
| |
| |

Write your answers down. Review each area of your life. Ask yourself these questions.

- What things are truly important to me in this area?
- How important are they currently?
- How are my relationships with others?
- What are my responsibilities?
- What is going well?
- What needs attention?
- What are my strengths in each area?
- What are my opportunities for growth?
- What must I do to lead a balanced life?
- How much money do I need?
- What, if anything, am I willing to give up?
- What are the possible consequences?
- Can I accept the consequences?

For each priority, imagine and visualize the best possible outcome. How will your business support you in these important aspects of your life?

How to Generate 100 Leads

Do you need help recognizing how many people you already know who could benefit from what you have to offer?

First

List everyone you know personally including friends, family, classmates, co-workers, neighbors, church members, school parents, committee members, service providers, current clients, lost leads, and so on.

This exercise alone should generate 100 leads.

Second

Create a mind map of all the people you know by separating them into categories, then think of all the people *they* know who they could introduce you to. For a demonstration of how to mind map, see *How to Map Your Mind* in the workbook.

Third

Review your Facebook, Linked In, Twitter and any other accounts you have on social media. Thoughtfully consider the social contacts you have on those applications. What larger groups are these people connected to? What problems do the groups have? How could you solve a specific problem for them?

Think … What Do They Want?

Look at your list of 100 people and think about what these people want. To make it easier, remember that most people want one or all of three very simple things:

- More time
- More money
- More love

Be sure to write down the product of your brainstorming session. This is valuable information.

If you have listed 100 people, and you have given some deep thought to the problems they are dealing with, you have laid the groundwork for the next exercise. The next exercise is a creative act of brainstorming to discover your unique market and the particular product or service you are uniquely qualified to provide to the market.

My Talents and Strengths

We are, each of us, born with innate talents that inform our interests through life. These "gifts" can be buried or disrespected, but they do not go away. Are you acknowledging and using all of your gifts?

Following and on the website are some third-party assessments to help you rediscover gifts you may have forgotten about or dismissed as not important. I find assessments like these to be useful tools for increasing self-awareness.

Some tools to help you rediscover your talents and interests are:

Strengths Finder 2.0: A business built on your personal strengths will be a more satisfying and possibly more successful business.

Strong Interest Inventory: This assessment must be administered by someone trained to do so. A Google search will reveal local resources.

Self-Directed Search: This is another career identification assessment. This one started me down my career path many years ago. Then it was a written questionnaire, now you can take it online for a small fee.

The latter two assessments are primarily intended for career exploration. If your interest is self-discovery, they have value but for identifying your ideal business. I prefer *Strengths Finder 2.0*.

My Character Strengths

You are more amazing than you think!

How Well Do You Know Your Own Strengths?

The business you choose will best enhance your sense of purpose and well-being to the extent that it allows you to daily exercise your personal strengths. You may be unaware of the strengths that your personal character gives you.

Learn About Your Strengths

For a simple assessment to help you recognize the value of your inherent characteristics, consider completing this *free online assessment* offered by the VIA Institute on Character.

The basic report is free. However, the real value of gaining awareness of your strengths is in the opportunity to explore how your strengths have served you in the past and how you can best apply your strengths to the creation of your desired life and business.

Think about your values and what you know about yourself. Which of your character strengths will you use in your business?

For a sneak preview of the strengths you will find within yourself, you can view an informative graphic on the website.

Tools for Brainstorming

We all have habitual ways of thinking. However, our brains are capable of thinking in several different ways. You help yourself to gain insight and attract original ideas when you *consciously* choose to think differently about a particular problem.

In this case, you will be using a creative thinking technique to think about the "problem" of what business is best for you.

Lateral Thinking

Edward de Bono originated the idea of "lateral thinking" and wrote the book *Six Thinking Hats* in 1985. It is from this book that the following ideas are derived.

You do not need to physically change hats. You do, however, need to consciously choose to practice a different style of thinking in order to unearth different insights. To expand your possibilities, consciously consider your business possibilities from the following points of view (Hats):

Information (White Hat)

Consider purely what information is available. What are the facts you know about your business possibilities? Consider, also, what information is missing.

Emotions (Red Hat)

Check in with your intuitive or instinctive gut reactions. State your emotional feeling about your entrepreneurial ambitions. When you think in this way you can express fears, likes, dislikes, loves, and hates.

Judgment (Black Hat)

Play the devil's advocate. Spot the weaknesses, difficulties, and logical inconsistencies with your vision.

Optimistic (Yellow Hat)

Be happy. Look for all the good in the world as it relates to your business idea. Identify the benefits, acknowledge the value, and accentuate the positive.

Creativity (Green Hat)

Explore the possibilities, alternatives, and unusual ideas. Be creative. Look for something that has never been done before.

Process Control (Blue Hat)

This hat is the compliance police. Some of these ways of thinking will be unnatural for you and therefore uncomfortable. Do it anyway. Put on the blue hat and check your work. Did you give effort to each way of thinking?

What new ideas have you discovered?

WRITE IT DOWN

How to Map Your Mind

One valuable business planning tool I use is mind mapping. Try using this completely free organizational and creativity tool to explore and expand your thinking.

This tool is infinitely useful; that is why I love this tool. The "rules" are flexible so feel free to improvise and adapt. There are many useful, instructional videos available on the Internet. Feel free to search around and see what you can learn.

What Is a Mind Map?

A mind map is a graphical diagram used to represent words, ideas, tasks, or other items. Each word is linked to and arranged around a central key word or idea.

Why Mind Map?

The value in a mind map is in its graphical, nonlinear design. A mind map allows you to capture tangential ideas and place them somewhere where they will stay put to analyze by grouping related concepts. Best of all, you can see it all on one page. This ability to keep adding ideas while not being tied to a linear progression is more creative, inclusive, and flexible than outlining.

British author and educator, Tony Buzan, claims to have invented it and codified the rules. I provide the following "rules." Read them over to see how to play the game and then take what you need and leave the rest.

Rules are made to be broken.

—Anonymous

The Seven "Rules" of Mind Mapping

1. Start in the center of a landscape page.
2. Use an image or picture for your central idea.
   The central idea is a concept. It is the topic around which all other ideas cluster. Using images to symbolize your concept is encouraged because images make the information more interesting and more memorable. Also, drawing will tap into the wisdom of the right side

of your brain. By all means, add images if you want but do not avoid mind mapping because you are not artistic or you do not have the time to find the right image.

3. Use colors throughout.

    I do use color. I find colors help categorize and emphasis. I like color. And there is something just fun and more creative about breaking out my magic markers.

For the rest of the "rules," a picture is worth 1,000 words. Since I recommend the use of color and this book is in black and white, you can find colorful examples on my website.

The other rules are:

1. Connect main branches to the central image and second level branches from the ends of main branches and third level branches from the end of the second level and so on.
2. Make branches curve and flow.
3. Use just one word per line and make the lines the same length as the word.
4. Use images throughout.

Need More Information?

No. You do not really but, if you want it anyway, here are some resources. There are books, software, and YouTube videos available. I use *NovaMind Pro* to build my maps but there are other programs available (*Xmind, Mindomo, MindMeister*). Some are even free. But do not get caught up in the details. The real value is in capturing what is in your mind. You will learn more if you just jump in and try it.

So, what is in your mind?

WRITE IT DOWN

_____

_____

_____

_____

How to Overcome Self-Limiting Beliefs

Is It True?

A limiting belief is simply a belief that is not true. We all hold ideas, often formed in childhood when we did not fully understand the complexity of the world, that are not absolutely true. Even as adult humans, our perception is limited. What we see and the ideas we form about what we see, do not necessarily reflect reality.

William Bridges, author of *Transitions: Making Sense of Life's Changes*, tells a story of interviewing for a job. He was confident and enthusiastic. He was sure he was perfect for the position. In the interview, he shared with the committee his ideas about turning the organization into a "life-transition center."

"They seemed interested," Bridges remembers. "One of them said that the other candidates hadn't had any ideas like that."

Sure in his mind that he was perfect for the position, Bridges left the interview with confidence and made plans to begin his new job. It was not until he heard they had chosen another candidate that he recognized the possible error in his perceptions of the meaning behind what he saw.

Often our understanding of reality is not challenged in such clear ways. Often it is up to us to recognize when we are limiting ourselves with ideas that are not necessarily true (Figure 3.3).

Five Clues to Help You Identify Limiting Beliefs

I cannot because….	For example:
It's hopeless	I do not have the money (It's hopeless)
I'm helpless	I am not good with money (I am helpless)
It's useless	It's a competitive field (It's useless)
I am blameless	The economy is bad (I am blameless)
I am worthless	I do not know how (I am worthless)

Figure 3.3 Identifying limiting beliefs

Self-Limiting Beliefs

When you have identified a limiting belief (Mine is: If I put myself "out there" in the public arena, I will be misunderstood and criticized. I am helpless), begin by questioning the validity of that belief.

I am not good with money (I am helpless).
ASK: How can I take charge?
I do not have the money (It's hopeless).
ASK: How is it possible?
It's a competitive field (It's useless).
ASK: How have others succeeded?
The economy is bad (I am blameless).
ASK: How can I be responsible?
I do not know how (I am worthless).
ASK: What if I deserved this?

Turn It Around

The Work

Byron Katie uses this technique in *The Work*. As Katie uses it, the work is "a way to understand what is hurting you, and to address the cause of your problems with clarity." If you suffer (don't we all?), you may want to explore her technique more deeply.

Instructions in using the technique are available for free on her website.

I discovered that when I believed my thoughts, I suffered, but that when I did not believe them, I did not suffer, and that this is true for every human being. Freedom is as simple as that.

—Byron Katie

Here we are going to use Katie's *"Four Questions"* to examine your limiting thoughts about the possibilities for your business:

Four Questions

If you have identified a limiting thought, ask yourself these questions.

1. Is it true? (Yes or No. If "no," move to 3)
2. Can you absolutely know that it's true? (yes or no)
3. How do you react, what happens, when you believe that thought?
4. Who would you be without the thought?

There is more, deeper self-awareness available using this technique. Deep personal and emotional self-reflection is valuable but beyond the immediate scope of this book. Feel free to explore *The Work* on your own.

Your Mission Statement

Mission Statements Can Be Controversial

In 2010, a school district in America became bogged down in a debate about their mission to "en-culturate" students into a democracy. The debate centered on the difference between en-culturate and indoctrinate.

Mission Statements Can Be Vague and Flowery

"Yahoo powers and delights our communities of users, advertisers and publishers——all of us united in creating indispensable experiences and fueled by trust."

Mission Statements Can Be Uninspiring

Pharmaceutical manufacturer Bristol-Myers' mission is:

"To discover, develop and deliver innovative medicines that help patients prevail over serious diseases."

Mission Statements Can Be Sassy

Richard Branson recommends writing a mission statement that sound like a heraldic motto. Something short enough to fit on a shield below the coat of arms. His suggestion for Virgin:

"Screw it, let us do it."

Why You Need a Mission Statement

The value of a mission statement for the startup entrepreneur is in helping you clarify your intentions. Specifically, what it is your business hopes to accomplish *for your customers*? From your clear understanding of what it is your business does, and who it serves, will flow the nut and bolts of your business plan. A good Mission Statement is important.

If you can answer the following questions, you should be able to state your purpose in a few sentences.

Questions to think about:

- Why will customers buy your product or service?
- What is your company committed to providing its customers?
- What can your company promise?
- What passions are you trying to satisfy by building this business?
- What is your product or service?
- What differentiates you from your competition?
- Describe your ideal customer.
- Why will customers buy this product or service?
- What value does this product or service provide the customer?
- What unique benefits does this product or service provide the customer?
- What passions are you trying to satisfy by building this business?
- What beliefs do you have about business that will impact this business?
- What is the highest good this business can achieve?
- What value will drive this business?
- Who will benefit from this business?

When you have done your thinking, complete this mission statement worksheet

WRITE IT DOWN

Mission Statement Worksheet

Your mission statement should be short and memorable. Aim to describe your target market and the benefit of your product in eight words or less. Ask yourself these questions:

- Why does your business exist?
- What makes your business unique?
- What do you provide for your customers?
- Why do people buy what you are selling?
- What is their urgent need? What are they moving away from?
- What are their compelling desires? What are they moving toward?
- What do you offer that is an investable opportunity for your target market?
- What are the deeper benefits of your product? (i.e., freedom, pride, and confidence)
- What is the highest good your business can achieve?
- What values will drive your business?
- Does your mission support your vision?

CHAPTER 4

Crafting a Business Vision From Your Mission

That which cannot be measured cannot be achieved.

—Locke and Latham

By now you should have a picture of your skills and your business mission and at least a vague idea of the business you intend to build. If you have done the exercises in this book and at the end of each chapter with honest sincerity up to this point, you must be excited about the possibilities ahead of you. That is great! You need to keep your eyes on the horizon and the future to come, but you also need to keep your feet on the ground because now it is time to convert your personal vision and your business mission into a working business plan.

A business plan—as in having a plan for your business—begins with your clear vision of the potential of your mission for your business. Your vision is a goal-oriented picture of what you intend to accomplish by completing your mission successfully. Once you are clear on your vision and mission, the plan for your business will begin to reveal itself. Your plan will specify your business objectives along with the strategies you will employ to meet those objectives and the actions you will take to make your idea a profitable reality. In this chapter, we will clarify your real-world vision for your business.

Your business vision should be different from, but not in conflict with, your vision for your life. You will know your vision and mission are clear when you can communicate what you see as well as what you plan to do in one brief statement.

Feet on the Ground

Your vision should be powerful and inspiring, but it also needs to be achievable. So ... for one more time, let us revisit your current reality.

See yourself creating and leading the business you have envisioned. Ask yourself the question, "If I could have this business right now, would I take it?"

Regardless of what your business idea is, it is definitely going to require a lot of work—hard work. It may require long hours, an investment of your life savings, or possibly relocating closer to your market. If your vision requires any of those potential changes, are you willing make such sacrifices? This is a very important question, and it goes to the deeper reasons for your existence. Make sure you take plenty of time and consider your answers carefully.

> *This planet doesn't need more 'successful people' but is in desperate need of more peacemakers, healers, restorers, storytellers and lovers of every shape and form. It needs people who live well in their places. It needs people of moral courage willing to join the fight to make the world habitable and humane. And these needs have very little to do with success—the way our culture sees it.*
>
> —David Orr

Be Honest About What You Value

I have worked extensively with a group of "wealth builders." I initially became involved with this group because I realized I had a lot of baggage about money. I was anxious and afraid about my ability to survive because I believed at some level that if I didn't have a full-time corporate job, I would be homeless and unloved.

At some point during one of my unemployed periods when I had time to do some self-reflection, I realized I really didn't know much about money. In fact, I believed that I was not a "numbers person." This idea may have become "truth" to me as a child when I failed 6th grade math. That was the only time in my life I ever failed a math class, but I internalized my failure. From that point on, I discounted any mathematical success I may have had. This is a typical brain-based human reaction. My closely held identity as "not good at math" was a self-limiting belief for me. (For more about how to overcome self-limiting beliefs, see the workbook materials at the end of Chapter 3.)

Even years later, I was still punishing myself for failing to grasp the "new math," a teaching technique introduced in the 1960s. I pretty much ignored my bank balance as long as there was enough money for groceries and my other modest wants and needs. The price I paid for this blissful ignorance was fear and uncertainty about my financial future accompanied by the not-necessarily-true idea that I must work a corporate job in order to survive.

When I realized my willful ignorance about how to manage money was causing my anxiety, I found a teacher and became deeply involved, both emotionally and financially, in learning how to make money work for me. My goal was to become wealthy. Sound familiar?

The experience of consciously deciding to become a millionaire definitely made a difference in my life. For a while, I was wealthy but being wealthy did not feel like I thought it would. The effort to invest wisely carried with it the same fear, uncertainty, and sense of not being good enough (how much money is enough?) as my disappointing career.

Then, with the 2007 economic meltdown in America, I was no longer wealthy and I had developed some serious regrets. I blamed myself for my risk taking, for my gullibility and for my greed. I blamed myself for endangering my family's future. I grew stressed, angry, self-critical, and even more anxious about my finances. I watched as people I knew—the same aggressive wealth builders whose advice I valued and whose methods I tried to model—went bankrupt. Their fabulous real estate holdings turned to dust, lawsuits sprouted like mushrooms, and banks suddenly took control of their lives.

In the end, I did not remain a millionaire for very long. Fortunately, I manage to survive well enough despite the financial setbacks of the recession.

Fast forward to seven years later, and I am in Johannesburg where (through what I thought was remarkable serendipity) I reconnected with the group of wealth building gurus I once admired and modeled myself after. I was surprised to find that though my own understanding of the value of wealth had changed, theirs had not.

Listening to the same message that had once lured me into the world of wealth building seven years earlier, I now had my own painful experiences to guide me. This time I saw their teachings as nothing more than "big talk." In reality, these self-styled, wealthy millionaires were not living an attractive life. In reality, they were flying around the world almost constantly. They were away from home much of the time and chronically jet lagged. They were working long days selling their wealth building programs in order to make more and more money. In fact, they were actually working very hard and sacrificing many important things that make life worthwhile such as time with family, close personal relationships, and contentment with what they already had. They certainly were not living the "good life" of the wealthy, at least not how I thought it would be.

"I do not watch television," bragged one of them. "I'd rather be making money." To this I ask, "Why? Why make more and more money? Is money an end in itself?"

To be clear, I am not advocating more television watching nor am I against making money. After all, I *want* you to build a business that makes money! I am just encouraging you to examine your relationship with money. Where is your heart in making money? What is your purpose in making money? Where is your connection to the larger world? What is the true value of money to you?

Before you agree to do whatever it takes to make money, give some thought to the true meaning of that money. The conclusion you reach in defining true value will be an individual definition that is uniquely yours. There is no right or wrong answer; there is only the answer that is right for *you*.

You will find additional, thought-provoking resources in the workbook materials.

Can Money Buy Happiness?

As you examine your relationship with money, go back to the factors that create true happiness:

- Work that is both enjoyable and challenging
- Close relationships with family and friends

- Good health
- A positive, optimistic outlook
- A strong belief in yourself

Can you create a business vision that will create wealth *and* give you these things as well?

If your answer to that question is "no," go back to Chapter 2 and revisit your personal vision. Remember, you can have it if you really want it but you may not be ready yet. Instead, just start right where you are and realize that every step is a learning process. Be honest with yourself. Be gentle with yourself. Be true to yourself.

Now ask yourself the same question about your business idea once more, "If I could have it now, would I take it?"

If the answer is a sincere "yes," then it is time to clarify a powerful and motivating business vision and set some serious, action-oriented goals to begin the process of building the business you can imagine.

However, if the answer is "no," revisit the exercises and create another mission and business vision that *does* work for you.

> *It is not enough to do your best; you must know what to do, and then do your best.*
>
> —Edward Deming

Head in the Sky: Your Business Vision Statement

Now it is time to define specifically your business vision.

The word vision has an ethereal connotation. Saints fasting in the desert have visions. Young people alone in the wilderness seek visions. Mystics and aesthetics have visions. This is *not* the type of vision you need for your business but if that type of vision comes to you, do not discount it! Your business vision should be a clear and concrete picture of the business you intend to have—right here on this earth *and* in the near future.

What Is a Vision Statement?

Your vision of your business is a vision of what is still ahead. It is a description of what your business will become in the future. That future may be

3, 5, or 10 years out. It is your vision that will keep you pointed in the right direction. That is why I believe it is important to be clear about not only what you want from your business but also how you want your business to contribute to your life.

Remember, a mission statement explains the *purpose* of your business, It tells why your business exists: what it does, for whom and how. The question you seek to answer with your mission statement is: Who do I serve and how do I serve them? These two aspects of a business plan, your vision and mission statements, are by far the hardest to pin down. That is why we will continue to draft and redraft your vision and mission. Each time you write down your thoughts you will be getting closer and closer to clarity.

Which Comes First?

Which comes first, vision or mission? This is actually a controversial question often debated from both sides. In reality, vision and mission often occur (at least evolve) more-or-less simultaneously. This is my preference. You many have a vision of a business that is grand and inspiring but your talents, aptitudes, and interests may lead you to a business that, while satisfying, has little potential to become huge. As you work through iteration after iteration of both your personal and business vision and mission, you will draw closer and closer to a balance of the two until, finally, you begin to uncover a truly inspiring and meaningful plan for your business and your life.

As you begin to build your business, keep your vision simple and meaningful to you. Do not be seduced by big corporate, high-level statements. At this point, your vision does not need to motivate your staff, impress your banker, or advance your brand. Your vision is *your* vision of *your* future business. Its purpose is to motivate and inspire *you* to create a business to support the lifestyle you described in your earlier personal vision.

This focused rewrite of your life vision into a business vision is step one of creating a working business plan. As I use the term, a business plan is just that—a *plan* for your business. It is not a heavy, detailed document for your banker. It is a written plan for *you*. As you work though the rest of this, you will be creating a working document—a simple business plan—that will include your intentions for your business, your strategies for realizing your intentions, and a task list for creating your business in the real world.

The business plans I find most useful for small business leaders are limited to one page in length. That one-page plan should include brief descriptions in five specific areas:

- Vision
- Mission
- Objectives
- Strategy
- Actions

You can find a blank copy of this simple and practical business plan on my website.

I have helped many clients complete this one-page plan and, in most cases, the hardest parts to complete are the vision and mission sections. Once an aspiring business owner understands exactly what they are creating, the objectives, strategies, and action-oriented tasks fall easily into place. That's when the magic begins.

If you have worked through the thinking exercises in the book so far, the good news is you have already done the hard work of choosing a compelling and motivating *mission* for your business. Once you complete the following vision exercise, all you have left to do is *write down* your mental image of the reality you intend to create.

So, for one last time, let us revisit your personal vision from your Draft Vision #2. Using your deep desires as a baseline, summarize the big picture of what you want your business to become. You should:

- Describe what your business will look like in five years.
- Challenge yourself to do more than you believe you are capable of, but not so much that you cease to believe in the larger possibilities of your vision.
- Use words and images that convey your passion.
- Be specific.

For clarity about the difference between your personal vision and your business vision, see the exercises in the workbook at the end of this chapter.

Draft #1: Your Business Vision

WRITE IT DOWN

Now for some insight about how to rewrite your business vision into a powerful vision statement. All it really requires is some deep thinking and a bit of tweaking to the wording of your vision. For additional help see the exercise in the workbook.

Deep Thinking: Crafting Your Vision Statement

Remember, the difference between your vision and your mission is—your vision describes *where* you are going while your mission briefly describes what you will be *doing*.

I used to have my clients begin the process of building a business plan by creating a vision, but I have found that getting clear on the mission of the business first helps provide boundaries for the business vision. Similar to poetry, having constraints for the vision encourages creativity.

As you imagine the details of what you are building, consider your current reality and the work you feel called to do.

Everyone has been made for some particular work, and the desire for that work has been put into their hearts.

—Rumi

What Are You Building?

In the vision of your future business:

- What are your products or services?
- What is your company famous for?
- What is your role?
- How do you spend your time?
- How much money will you generate?

Whom Do You Know and Whom Do You Serve?

In your vision of your future business:

- Who are your customers? Describe three to five types of customers you will serve.
- Who are your peers?
- Who are the people you will meet to discuss your industry?
- Who are your partners?
- Who are your mentors?

Why Is Your Business Needed?

- Why are you creating this business? What is the value you share?
- What makes your customers choose your particular product? What is the value they receive?
- How will your personal values influence this business?
- What is your business philosophy?

Why You Need a Business Philosophy

Revisit the values exercise in Chapter 2 and determine which of your strongest held values will apply to your business. Right now the vision and mission you are developing is just for you. As your business grows, you will be creating an entire business subculture. Your business culture will be a combination of the values you hold dear along with the rules and guidelines you will develop into expected patterns of behavior within your business. If you begin honoring your values now, the culture you create will be one you are proud of and not one you will eventually need to change.

Ask yourself the following questions:

- As a business leader, what are my highest values?
- What are the contributions I want to make as a business leader?
- What makes me unique as a business leader?
- What are five words or phrases to describe my leadership style?
- How will people in different areas of my life describe their relationships with me?
- How am I building my circles of influence?
- How do I want to treat people in general?
- How do I approach and delegate tasks?
- What am I doing to continually build and improve my leadership capacity?
- What do I want my legacy to be?

Define your promises to yourself, to your customers, and to your future employees. Write it down.

WRITE IT DOWN

Business Vision Statement First Draft

Make your vision specific and measurable.

Following are examples of visions that are not specific or measurable statements. If the first draft of your statement is similar to the following ones, it's time to dig deeper.

To share our gift and change the world one person at a time

Gift? What gift? Change? What change? How will people know you have changed the world? How will you know you have changed even one person? What will they do differently? How will the world be different?

To raise awareness in business that "we all have customers"

How will you know when you have successfully "raised awareness"? What value will this improved awareness create? What problem will it solve? For whom? Who will pay to have their awareness raised?

Following are statements that are more specific and therefore easier to accomplish.

Within the next five years, ZZZ Tours will become the premier eco-tour company in _____. It will increase revenues to one million dollars in 2010 by becoming internationally known for the comfort and excitement of the whale-watching tours it offers.

Five years from now, Tiny Tots Diaper Service will be the top-grossing diaper service in the Lower Mainland by consistently providing a reliable, affordable service for parents with small children.

In the previous examples, each has a concrete measurement and a brief description of how it will be accomplished.

- "Revenues of one million" will be achieved through whale watching tours.
- "Top-grossing" business will happen through a reliable and affordable diaper service.

Avoid the temptation to relegate your vision to the realm of the visionary.

Never doubt that a small group of thoughtful committed citizens can change the world; indeed, it's the only thing that ever has.

—Margaret Mead

The beginning of a small group of thoughtful committed people starts with you. Take the time to write down your revised business vision now with words that are concrete, measurable, and clearly concise. If you need some additional guidance, you can find a helpful worksheet in the workbook.

Draft Business Vision #2

WRITE IT DOWN

When you are happy with your statement, complete the mission and vision portions of your one-page business plan. You will find a template on my website.

Next Steps

In the next chapter, we will turn our attention to creating a business model. Your business model is a picture of the system that is your key to profitability. The brainstorming you will do to capture your business model will take your idea from being just an inspiring vision to being one-step closer to a profitable reality. Are you not excited?

Module 4 Workbook—Crafting a Business Vision From Your Mission

Learning Objectives

- Gain a deeper understanding of your deeply held values around money.
- Develop clear and concise statements for the vision and mission of your business.
- Complete sections one and two of your plan for your business.

Your business vision describes your business as it will be in the future. Your vision should be powerful and inspiring, but it also needs to be achievable.

When you have completed these exercises, you will be ready to complete the first two sections—the hardest sections—of your plan for your business.

Information	For the love of money
Exercise	Brainstorm your business vision
Exercise	Personal vs. business vision
Tools	Simple business plan

Index to Exercises

For the Love of Money

These resources explore the effects of wealth on compassion, self-esteem, and society.

Note: For the record, I am not against wealth, success or profits. I am against greed, selfishness, and lack of compassion. What follows is merely information for your own personal self-examination of your relationship to money.

In my last year on Wall Street my bonus was $3.6 million—and I was angry because it was not big enough. I was 30 years old, had no children to raise, no debts to pay, no philanthropic goal in mind. I wanted more money for exactly the same reason an alcoholic needs another drink: I was addicted.

Excerpt from January 2014 New York Times article

In a series of startling studies, psychologists at the University of California at Berkeley have found that "upper-class individuals behave more unethically than lower-class individuals." Ongoing research is trying to find out what it is about wealth—or lack of it— that makes people behave the way they do.

Excerpt from April 2012 Scientific American article

Click here to read more about this research into the effect that wealth has on people's generosity and sense of connectedness.

Your Business Vision (First Draft)

WRITE IT DOWN

This (Figure 4.1) is a first draft. Write down your thoughts but do not worry about full sentences or complete ideas.

WHAT?	What is the business I am building? What are your products or services? What is your business famous for? What is your role? How do you spend your time?
WHERE?	What is your geographic service area? Where do your customers live? Do you have a specific brick and mortar location? Where?
WHO?	Describe three to five types of customers Who are your peers, the people you meet to discuss your industry, your partners? Who are your mentors?
WHEN?	When will your business be a reality? How will you know it is real?
WHY?	Why are you creating this business? What is the value you share? Why do your customers choose your product? What is the value they receive?
HOW?	How will our personal values impact this business?

Figure 4.1 Draft your business vision

My Business Vision Statement

Your Vision Statement (Figure 4.2) should describe your idea in a manner that captures these areas of your future business.

Within the next _____   grow   _____
                      (X years)   (Business name)

      into a   _____
                    (Annual sales)   (Description of business)

 providing   _____
                              (How you serve)

          to   _____
                              (Who you serve)

Figure 4.2 Your business vision statement

The Difference Between a Personal and Business Vision

As you may have gathered, I really don't want to see you enter into a business solely for the money. I want your business to support your fabulous life.

The following exercise (Figure 4.3) is designed to help you sort out for yourself the synergies between your personal vision and your business vision:

	In my personal life	In my business life
Things I really enjoy doing		
What brings me joy and happiness		
The two best moments of my past week		
Things I would do if I won the lottery		
Issues I care deeply about		
My most important values		
Things I am very, very good at		
Things I'd rather not do		

Figure 4.3 Personal vs. business vision

Write Three Drafts

- Write your first draft in the preceding format.
- Write your second draft using your own words.
- Write one more draft with no limits—think big.

Keep rewriting until you are comfortable that you have described your vision for your business. Do not obsess. You can and should revisit your plan regularly. When you are ready, enter your vision statement into the simple business plan template on the following pages.

WRITE IT DOWN

| |
| |
| |
| |

Your Simple Business Plan

Having a plan is the key to business success.

Every exercise in the book is intended to help you do the deep thinking necessary to clarify and simplify your understanding of your business. When you have done the hard thinking of a business leader, you will be ready to complete this simple, one-page plan (Figure 4.4). The value of this simple plan is you must be clear in order to keep it simple.

When you are ready, complete the mission and vision portions of this plan.

WRITE IT DOWN

| |
| |
| |
| |

Using a simple sheet of paper and a pen, limit yourself to two or three sentences and record in writing your business vision and your business mission.

Simple Business Plan

Your Business Name _____ **Last Updated:** _____

Vision

_____

Mission

_____

Objectives

_____

Strategies

_____

Action Plan

_____

Figure 4.4 Simple business plan

CHAPTER 5

Turning Your Business Vision Into a Profitable Business Model

Given your mission and your business vision, how does your business make money?

This is not a simple question, but it is a very important question … critical actually. No doubt, your business vision includes a certain level of wealth and status for you, the creator, but what about the relationship of your business to the larger world? How does your business create value? What is the service your business provides? Why is it important to your customers and clients?

The focus of this chapter is on getting a clear picture of the relationship between your desire to make money and your desire to create a worthwhile business that contributes to your community.

When I first decided to become an entrepreneur, my sole desire was to make money, preferably *a lot* of money, without working for someone else. My mission was vague, unfocused, and, frankly, selfish. My results reflected my intentions.

I started my journey to becoming an entrepreneur back in the height of interest in the *Law of Attraction* in America. I should have known better.

A Brief Explanation of the Law of Attraction

Simply put, the *Law of Attraction* claims that what we focus on expands. By focusing on positive or negative thoughts, one creates an emotional vibration that will attract similar vibrations: that is, positive thoughts attract positive results, negative thoughts attract negative results.

This belief is based on the idea that people and their thoughts consist of "pure energy." and that "like attracts like," meaning a certain kind of energy will attract the same kind of energy. Many people claim to have attracted wealth, love, and success simply through the power of the *Law of Attraction.*

When I was on my wealth-seeking quest, I very much wanted the *Law of Attraction* to be true. I wanted wealth to be accessible to me through my positive thoughts. The truth is, on some level, I have discovered that the law *is* true. After all, I achieved my freedom from my day job—twice—by thinking repeatedly with sincere conviction: "I hate this job!" Through the sheer force of my negative thoughts, I succeeded at having those hated jobs go away. Although the outcome I created was not the outcome I had consciously chosen, according to the law, I was responsible for my results. I should have carefully and clearly envisioned what I desired (a new way to make money) and then remained focused on the positive outcome I wanted to achieve (getting paid to do what I enjoyed) instead of my negative (I hate this job!) thoughts.

I can easily see where the power of this law worked in the negative realm for me. Where I find the promise of the *Law of Attraction* breaks down (for me) is in a lack of *consistently* yielding positive results. This seems to be true not only for me, a person who tends to be somewhat negative, but it is also true for many other people. No matter how positive one might be, life is still unpredictable.

Even so, the idea of attracting positive results through the power of one's thoughts has a long history. In my own field of neuroscience-informed coaching, I have seen that one's thinking does indeed have a great deal of power over one's results.

One positive thought that has served me well comes from a little book written in 1910 by American thinker Wallace Wattles. In his book, *The Science of Getting Rich*, Wattles advocates thinking clearly about what you want, but he also says:

> *By thought you can cause the gold in the hearts of men to be compelled toward you, but your personal activity must be such that you can rightly receive what you want when it reaches you. You are not to take it as charity, nor to steal it; you must give every man more in value than he gives you in cash value.*
>
> —Wallace Wattles

To illustrate his point, Wattles paints an amusing picture. Your thinking can fill your pockets with gold, he explains, but your thoughts will not cause the gold to rise out of the earth, roll down the hill, mint itself into coins, and leap into your pocket.

All along the journey, from raw ore to gold coin, someone has to work in order to add value. Someone extracts the raw product out of the earth itself, another person will transform the raw ore into pure metal, and a third person in the production process will mint the gold into coins.

When this minted coin finally nears your pocket through the power of your own positive thinking, you must exchange a fair value for all the processing the precious metal has gone through thus far. In other words, if you want a million dollars, you had better have something worth a bit more than a million dollars to offer in the exchange.

You must give every man more in value than he gives you in cash value.
—Wallace Wattles

I know this is a more sobering and less magical interpretation of the *Law of Attraction* than is often portrayed. Creating value is much harder than just sitting in your broken-down armchair diligently imagining it is the driver's seat of a Ferrari. This may be why this aspect of Wattles' thinking is so rarely emphasized in *Law of Attraction* circles. Still, I think his thinking may be the most important concept for an aspiring business builder. Once we accept personal responsibility for creating value in this world, we then have the possibility of accessing whatever wealth-creating power there may be in our positive thoughts.

Truly, you *can* get rich. Success *is* possible but it does not happen magically. You can make the money you want and need if, when that money actually arrives, you are ready to exchange something of value in return.

Your business's mission is to create value. The business model you will clarify in this chapter is a picture of how you intend to create that value. You will know you have successfully created a system that generates real value when your business begins to make money.

The Power of Intention

In *Made to Stick: Why Some Ideas Survive and Others Die,* authors Chip and Dan Heath talk about a military concept called "Commander's Intent." This clear and concise statement appears at the top of every military order specifying the goal and the desired end-state of the operation.

"You can lose the ability to execute the original plan," says a military officer, "but you never lose the responsibility of executing the intent."

The intent of your business is to make money, and you will do this while providing a valuable product, solving a problem, or improving people's lives. Your business intends to serve *and* make a profit. You must make a profit. Profit is essential in order to have the resources necessary to continue to serve more and more people. Building a profitable business is your own Commander's Intent, and you should never lose sight of it.

To achieve your desired profitable end state, you need a business model that clearly shows where the money will come from.

Your Business Idea Is Ready but Do You Know Where the Money Is Coming From?

You've done the preparations for your business, but are you ready? You may think you have a good business idea, but until you have developed a business model that shows where the money is coming from, you cannot be sure it will work.

Building a successful business is a complicated process.

One client of mine was clearly frustrated as he worked through these same difficult questions with me. He told me about a man he had heard about who made a fortune with his simple cable-tie business.

"That is what I want—just a simple business," my client sighed.

Unfortunately, there are very few simple businesses, at least not very many simple businesses that are also sufficiently profitable.

The Rest of the Story

In 2008, a British man received a substantial investment for his cable-tie business when he won a reality-television competition. The investment and publicity he received helped him land a multimillion euro contract for his cable-tie business.

The rest of this rags-to-riches story includes the fact that this 35-year-old man lived with his parents in their humble home. He had been living with his parents for 14 years while he worked on his simple business idea. Referring to his good fortune, he said, "My personal life—marriage and children—has suffered because I put all my energy into this."

Two years after the triumph of his television-propelled windfall, his product ran into legal issues regarding his patent. The company still exists today but nothing about this business success story is simple.

I doubt your vision includes living in your parents' basement. A solid business model will keep you out of perpetual dependency. With the development of a workable business model, you will turn your attention to the important aspect of business—making a reasonable profit. As you flesh out your business model, you will get a deeper understanding of your business mission. Your mission, the value you add to the universe, is the essence of the system you are creating.

What Goes Into a Business Model

According to author and entrepreneur Seth Godin, a business model should provide answers to four elemental questions:

- **Why Should People Give You Money?**
  Unbelievably, many businesses fail because considerable time and money are spent building a product nobody wants. You have already spent some time yourself thinking about your market and the problems you want to solve. Your business model must clearly communicate the value of your product to others. If you cannot convince your spouse, your best friend, or your banker of the value of your product, how will you be able to convince your customers?

  What value will you add to society through the transformational process of your business? Who will benefit from this transformation?
- **How Do You Contain Costs?**
  I have a client who wants to sell high fashion shoes to young women. She sees a need for attractive shoes in sizes that fall at

either end of the scale—for particularly small feet as well as unusually large feet. Her main challenge is to find a supplier who can supply the shoes she envisions at a price point that her market—young women—can afford. She may or may not be able to overcome this challenge, and until she finds a solution such as lower quality shoes, a higher quality market, or some other unique solution, she will not have a viable business model.

- **What Insulates You From Your Competitors?**
  Do you ever watch the Nature Channel? Like the world of predator and prey, the business world is red in tooth and claw. Your entry into the marketplace will not go unnoticed and the more successful you are, the more noticeable you will be. Like wild animals, your competition will not give up its territory without a fight, so, what is your plan to protect yourself from your competition?

  This is not as scary as it sounds. Some planning ahead of time will save you wasted effort in the long run. When I started placing my cappuccino vending machines in businesses, larger soft drink vendors quickly reacted. In my case, I had a unique product and my machines were smaller than the large vending machines commonly used at the time. These two advantages gave me flexibility as to the placement of my machines. Much to the annoyance of the large soda vendors, I was able to find a niche for my machines—literally.

  Knowing where your strengths lie can save you significant time and effort when fighting off challengers. You already have given thought to your personal strengths. What are the unique strengths of your business?

- **How Will People Find You in Order to Become Your Customers?**
  This is a make-or-break question because many unique market niches are hard to find. How does someone target a market group that is not actively seeking a solution? It is possible to build a tribe of loyal followers, but it takes many hours of marketing, hard work, and effort. Do you have the resources to stay in business while you find and recruit your customer base? Where will you find them? How will you communicate with them? You do not want to start building your business until you *know* you have a viable market.

I recently received an e-mail from a young South African man who had fallen on hard times. He had very little money but thought he could begin rebuilding by selling small items like fruit, cigarettes, and candy to commuters when they were on their way to work early in the morning.

His business plan included the items he would sell, the cost of his inventory, and his hopeful projections for profit, but he described his location vaguely as "somewhere." Without a solid understanding of where his small shop would be located, the traffic he could expect, and the level of demand the market would have for his product, he had little basis for his predictions of profit.

Other aspects you may want to have in the description of your business model include:

Revenue Streams What other streams are emptying into your pool of money? More than one source of revenue is best. We call these multiple streams of income. For example, a client of mine developed a cleaning service. Her competitive advantage was her "green" cleaning products. She was in a direct marketing company that allowed her business to claim a commission on all the cleaning products the company used. Voilá—multiple revenue streams!

Knowing your sources of income is the key to knowing what kind of business you are in. The founder of McDonalds famously claimed that he was not in the fast food industry but in the real estate business instead. Knowing what you do in order to create the income you desire is the key to knowing what is most important for you to do each day.

Partnerships Who else is in your business with you such as vendors, employees, government entities, suppliers, distributors, or affiliates, and so on?

Additional Resources It is important to know where your materials are coming from because there may well be more to your business than you realize. Even a simple idea, like cable ties or office cleaning services, is not necessarily a simple business. Think of the resources required to produce just one plastic cable tie. It takes chemicals, molds, manufacturing equipment, shipping containers, and quality control measures, just to name a few. Think of all the personnel, supplies, and equipment that are involved with a simple cleaning business. What other resources do you need for your business?

Channels of Distribution How does your product get to your customer? Cable ties ship from a factory, but how does the customer find the product that will solve his cable organization problem? Will customers purchase the product at a brick-and-mortar retail store or at an online store? Or, will your primary channel of distribution be through a partnership with an electronics manufacturer?

For the green cleaning business, cleaning supplies are required, employees must arrive on time, and they have to be fully equipped on site. What business system ensures the entire process happens seamlessly each and every time?

How to Design a Business Model

Developing a business model is similar to trying to resolve any messy problem that lacks a clear understanding. When it comes to communicating your vision through a business model, a picture truly is worth a thousand words.

We are about to explore a development tool known as "Rich Picture." A rich picture is a way to explore, acknowledge, and define a situation or a system. The technique consists of drawing a picture of a complex situation to help to create a mental model. When you draw a picture of your business, you make clear outside of your head what may or may not be clear inside your head.

As a business development tool, a rich picture is a cartoon-like representation of your business model. A complete rich picture will identify all the elements of your business already mentioned along with the stakeholders and their concerns, issues, or objectives, together with some of the structure underlying the activities required to add value to your raw materials. When you can draw such a picture of the business vision in your mind, you will be able to communicate your vision in a way that will motivate and inspire others.

How to Draw a Rich Picture of Your Business

- Start with one large sheet of blank white paper.
- Use pictures, symbols, keywords, cartoons, or sketches that can accurately display scenes or images that represent the parts of your business.
- Use as many colors as you like.

A rich picture is an attempt to assemble *everything* that might be relevant to your business all in one place—in this case, the "place" being one sheet of paper. It will also conceptualize the transformational process that creates the value of your business. (*Note*: For a valuable visual explanation of the Rich Picture process, see the resources on the website.)

To explain the process of creating a rich picture we will use the analogy of the process of minting ore into gold coin.

Imagine gold ore rolling down a hill helped along the way by miners, transport drivers, and other resources until it teeters on the edge of a circle. This circle represents the boundaries of your business. You and your business intend to take the raw gold ore and transform it into gold coin. Within the circle is your value-added, transformational process. As the raw ore passes through to the other side of your circle, the gold will be changed in an important way, a way that is valuable to your customers. So ... what is your process? Think it through by drawing a picture.

Step One

Draw a circle to represent the boundaries of your business process.

Outside of the circle, on the left-hand side, draw or place pictures or symbols that represent all of the resources and information your business

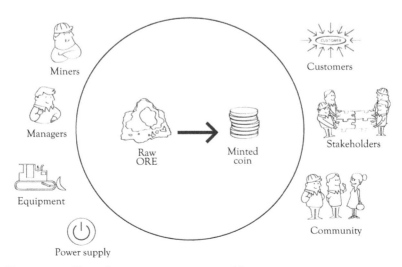

Figure 5.1 Transforming raw ore into gold coin

process requires as inputs. Think about such things as raw materials, resources, capital input, vendors, and so on.

On the right-hand side, outside of the circle, draw symbols to represent the elements that receive value from your business: your customers, stakeholders, investors, and the wider community, and so on (Figure 5.1).

Figure 5.1 Transforming Raw Ore Into Gold Coin

Represent every aspect of your business inputs and valuable outputs you can think of. Use words if you must, but try to convert your words to simple pictures. Pictures are engaging, memorable, and open to a wider and possibly more creative interpretation.

Remember, your business is a transformational process. You will picture that transformation on paper.

Step Two

On the inside of your business boundary circle, place symbols that represent all the people, processes, and activities that you need to accomplish your transformational process. Possibilities include: partnerships, distribution systems, equipment, employees, and the activities required to complete the transformation process.

Think about each system or process at a high level. For example, I once owned a coffee business. I can tell you that to transform coffee beans and milk into a hot, foaming cappuccino you will need coffee beans and milk from vendor partnerships. You will need equipment in the form of an espresso machine and water. You will need a distribution system that includes cups. You will need to hire a barista and train that person to perform the task of brewing the coffee and foaming the milk.

You can see the process of brewing espresso is, when broken down, detailed and complex. Your goal in this exercise is to picture your *entire* business model on one sheet of paper. To do this you will need to keep your symbols broad. Pictures help.

For the purposes of your first, high-level picture of your business, you do not want to sketch your processes down to the level of tamping down the grounds in the filter. Instead, only picture the activity of brewing a cappuccino. You can create another more detailed picture when the exact brewing process information becomes relevant.

Choose a symbol or a sketch for every aspect of your business model that has occurred to you so far in the process of developing your business plan. Use words only if a sketch or some other imagery is not possible.

For an example, let's look at the internal business process of transforming gold ore into gold coins (Figure 5.2).

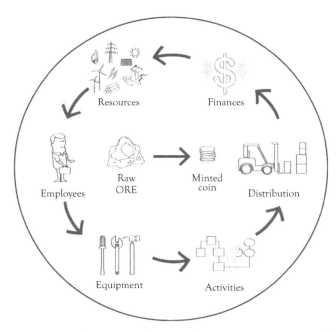

Figure 5.2 Internal processes for transforming raw ore into gold coin

Figure 5.2 Internal Processes for Transforming Raw Ore Into Gold Coin

Take the time to include all aspects of your business at its highest level but take care not to over think it. That kind of in-depth analysis will come later in the process. For now, use the techniques of mind-mapping and whatever natural artistic skills you have in order to create a symbolic picture of your business idea.

Picture Your Process

Use action verbs and arrows to create the big picture of the *activities* necessary to develop your system. The objective is to sketch out the actions and interactions that will take place within your business.

Use Verbs

Remember you are building a system—not just a job. It is important to avoid describing the necessary tasks. Instead, describe your high-level business processes with pictures or, if you must use words, use verbs. Verbs will help you think of the *transformations* that must occur in order to realize your vision for your business. Try to keep it simple with between five and seven "bubbles" of action depicted.

Use Arrows

The arrows (Figure 5.3) show the logical dependency and connection of all of the actions that make up the transformation involved with turning your business idea into an actual business.

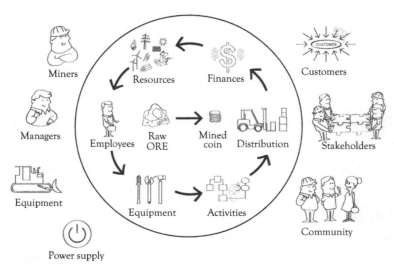

Figure 5.3 Rich picture of a value added process

The purpose here is to create a drawing of the mental model of your business vision. Your picture should be clear to anyone you choose to share it with.

Figure 5.3 Rich Picture of a Value-Added Process

Now You Try It

Begin by writing out either your mission statement or a clear statement of the problem you intend to solve for your particular market niche.

WRITE IT DOWN

Next, make a list all of your stakeholders and take care to include everyone who has a reason to care if your business succeeds or fails.

WRITE IT DOWN

Brainstorm and list all of the keywords that are relevant to your business. Do not analyze or be particular about the keywords you come up with at this point. Just write down everything you can think of.

WRITE IT DOWN

Your Rich Picture should contain all of the relevant and necessary concepts for your business in the form of pictures and/or symbols. The value of drawing a picture is primarily because a picture can communicate more information than words. You may use descriptive labels if necessary, but do not make your picture too "wordy."

- Identify the actors.
- Identify the activities.
- Identify the resources needed for each activity.
- Identify the flow of resources.
- Draw a boundary around the individual systems that create your business.

Being able to draw a clear picture of your business model will help you recognize the players in your system, the various processes needed, and how and where you create value. Creating value and exchanging that value for money is the essence of your business model. It should include:

The Value

When you understand your processes and the wholesale cost to you, you will be able to establish the value of your product.

The Transformation

The transformation created by your business adds value. Your market will gladly exchange money for the value you added. The difference between your costs and the value your market assigns is your profit.

A clear picture of the entire system that is your business model is your starting point for developing a detailed understanding of each activity and process that will ultimately create your value-added transformation.

Using this template (Figure 5.4), describe your business model.

WRITE IT DOWN

MY BUSINESS IS A SYSTEM TO:

BY MEANS OF   WHAT

IN ORDER TO ACHIEVE   HOW

WHY

A

TRANSFORMATION

IN WHICH

ACTORS DO WHAT

FOR

CUSTOMERS

Figure 5.4 Business model template

Use this information to rewrite the mission portion of your simple business plan.

Are you still struggling with your business plan at this point?

If your answer is yes, do not worry too much about it. Most entrepreneurs have so many good ideas that it can be hard to see the forest (the big picture of a single business plan) because of the trees (all the great business ideas).

For more information as well as step-by-step instructions on how to complete your own picture of your business model, see the informative video on my website.

On the other hand, people have different ways of thinking and learning; maybe visual illustrations (pictures) are just not helpful to you personally. If pictures are not your thing, try a different exercise for defining your business model. For an in-depth but simple checklist for developing a unique business model, see the C.A.T.W.O.E. exercise in the workbook at the end of this chapter. Once completed, this simple, yet thought-provoking checklist will help you create a concise model for your business.

Next Steps

At this point, you have completed the first, and by far the most difficult, thinking about your business. Now that you have a very clear picture of your business model, you should be able to complete both the vision and mission statement parts of your simple business plan with statements that are clear to others and also rich with meaning for yourself.

You now have a clear "Commander's Intent." it is time to move on to the fun, action-oriented part of business planning. This is where you move from being a visionary to being a strategizing and action-oriented entrepreneur.

Are you ready? Then let us do this!

Module 5 Workbook—Turning Your Business Vision Into a Profitable Business Model

Learning Objectives

- Recognize the importance of adding value through a transformational process.
- Use self-understanding, visioning and your understanding of your mission to develop a clear, visual picture of the business you will build.
- Recognize clearly the monetary value of the business process you envision.

This is it! This is where you develop a plan for making a profit.

Information	More about the Law of Attraction
Video	How to draw a rich picture
Tool	C.A.T.W.O.E.

Index to Exercises

More About the Law of Attraction

If you are not familiar with the belief that by focusing on positive or negative thoughts one can bring about positive or negative results, I encourage you to do some research. The idea behind this theory of possibility has some validity. And the ideas are now a significant part of the "Wealth Coaching" culture.

The Internet, particularly YouTube, is full of entertaining resources to help you familiarize yourself the *Law of Attraction*.

For an overview of where it all began, the full movie, *The Secret*, is available for free on You Tube. Go to www.youtube.com and search *The Secret*. You will find several offerings from which to choose.

Oprah discovered *The Secret* and the *Law of Attraction (LOA)* in 2007. YouTube is full of videos of her and various celebrities discussing their results. Search "Oprah" and "LOA" or *Law of Attraction*. Other deeper and more interesting resources include Napoleon Hill's book, *Think and Grow Rich* and, as mentioned, my personal favorite, *The Science of Getting Rich,* by Wallace Wattles.

In the next exercise you will be drawing a detailed picture of your business. As you do, you will be attracting to you what you envision.

How to Draw a Rich Picture of Your Business

Complete written instructions are provided in this chapter. You may also view video instructions on the website.

C.A.T.W.O.E.

If you are having trouble seeing your business system in clear detail, try this thinking exercise adapted from work by Peter Checkland and Brian Wilson of Lancaster University.

WRITE IT DOWN

This tool is, in essence, a simple checklist to help with your thinking. Ask and carefully answer, in one sentence the following questions about all aspects of your business:

Customer

Customers (the recipient of the output of the transformation, the victim, the beneficiary)

- Who is on the receiving end?
- What problems do they have now?
- How will they react to what you are proposing?
- Who wins, who loses?

Actors

Actors (individuals who will do the activities)

- Who will do the work
- What do they want?
- How might they react?

Transformational Process

Transformation process (value-added conversion)

- What is the process for transforming inputs into outputs?
- What are the inputs, where do they come from?
- What are the outputs? Where do they go?
- What are the steps in between?

World View

Weltanschauung (statement of belief about the purpose, aim, wider good, the world)

- What is the bigger picture into which your business fits?
- What are the real problems in this picture?
- What is the wider impact of your solution?

Owner

Owner (wider-system, decision maker with authority over the system)

- Who is the real owner of the process?
- Can they help you or stop you?
- What would cause them to get in your way?
- What would lead them to help you?

Environmental Constraints

Environmental constraints (external to the system)

- What are the broader constraints that act upon your idea?
- What are the limits: ethical, legal, financial, resources, regulations, and so on?

CHAPTER 6

Owning Your Business: Strategy and Objectives

Leadership is the capacity to translate vision into reality.
—Warren Bennis

Armed with a clear picture of your business model, you should now be ready to get quite clear about your intentions. As Commander of your business, you are in a position to know which outcomes are most urgently required to reduce the tension between your current reality and your vision. Your leadership task is to develop a strategy to realize your intentions.

Know the Territory

The standard tool for analyzing the territory you must conquer is the SWOT analysis. SWOT stands for Strengths, Weaknesses, Opportunities, and Threats.

It can be difficult to know just what opportunities and dangers lurk in the dark woods that is your marketplace, especially for a new business builder, but you need to learn as much you can about your particular business niche. The more you know about the territory, the more prepared you will be to overcome any challenges that come along.

Give particular attention to your strengths. While it is good to be aware of the threats and risks you may face, your most successful defense tactics will come from your strengths.

Business Strengths

I hope that you have explored and are confident with your personal strengths. Now it is time to think about strengths once again. Only this time, think about the strengths of your business in particular.

As you analyze your *business* strengths, consider the following areas:

Experience

You know what you know. Do not discount the power of your personal expertise and experience. We all tend to think of ourselves as less competent than our peers are, but that is more a function of your self-protecting brain then it is reality. Review your skill set (from Chapter 3) as it compares your competition. You have a strength that they do not have. Find it. Exploit it.

Location

How is the location of your business an asset? If it is not a competitive advantage already, how could it become an asset?

Product Quality

What makes your product or service superior to what your competition has to offer? Your quality advantages need to include more than just your price. How can you maximize the unique traits you bring to your business and your product? For an exercise to help you brainstorm about these unique benefits, see the workbook.

Flexibility

The ability to respond quickly to changes in the environment is a distinct advantage of a small business. Think about the small roofing companies whose simple structure enables them to respond quickly to repair needs after a destructive storm. How could business flexibility open new markets for your company?

Team

Who is on your team? What strengths do they bring to the table? What new strengths can you add to your business through strategic partnerships?

Creative Advantage

In this book, you have access to all of the tools you might need to expand or adapt your business ideas until you pinpoint exactly what market advantage will open the door to your dreams. Just keep your thought processes working as you consciously pursue your creative insights.

In the workbook, you will find two additional thinking exercises to help you identify the unique strengths of your business.

Weaknesses

You may have heard the world is not always fair. Somewhere someone in a similar business has some advantage over you, fair or unfair. You need to identify this advantage and then figure out creative ways to either adopt or counteract the advantage so that it will not negatively affect your business. In the workbook, the Ideation Exercise can guide you through the thinking process it will take in order to analyze any advantages your competitors might hold over you.

If you are not exactly sure what areas you may need to work on to improve your chances of business success, see the business challenge checklist in the workbook.

Opportunities

In Chapter 3, you identified a problem and a group of individuals who would benefit from your solution to their problem. This is an opportunity for you to pursue. Are there any other opportunities you can identify?

Threats

What do you need to watch out for? Threats can be external like the economy, unexpected competition, a change in demographics, and so on. Threats can also be internal such as time constraints, lack of commitment, or interference from others. Once you have identified the potential challenges you may face, you will be better prepared to confront them.

List (Figure 6.1) each of your business strengths, weaknesses, opportunities, or threats.

WRITE IT DOWN

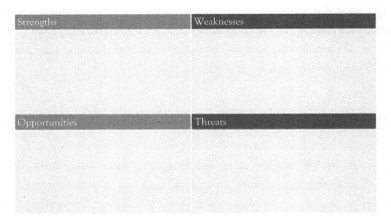

Figure 6.1 SWOT analysis

One of the challenges for a strategic business leader (like you) is to use your strengths in order to discover innovative solutions to overcoming any challenges or weaknesses that exist. For example, in the early stages of development, Google had to overcome the challenge of how to make money when their search engine product was free. Even though their original pricing model was a weakness, their strength of huge numbers of users provided a strategy to overcome that weakness. Their innovative solution of "pay-per-click" made Google into a household verb. How many times have you heard the suggestion to just "Google it" when you were looking for an answer or solution to some question or problem? They definitely overcame their pricing challenge!

Now ... what opportunities can *you* discover as you seek innovative strategies for overcoming the challenges you have identified for your own business?

What Your Business Plan Has to Do With Getting the Lifestyle You Want

Applying all of your creative energies to the question of what business opportunities to pursue is important. Once you have completed your

SWOT analysis, you will be able to identify the outcomes that are most important for realizing your vision and mission.

Your answer to the question, "How shall we pursue this opportunity?" will become your strategy. A good strategy will bring you the lifestyle you imagine, while a wrong strategy can spell failure.

A leader is one who knows the way, goes the way, and shows the way.

—John Maxwell

Objectives, Strategies, and Tasks

Your intent, as Commander, is to accomplish your vision using your selected strategy. You pursue your strategy by setting strategic objectives. You accomplish your goal as you reach each objective. You will progress one-step at time; you will conquer one hill at a time.

My clients often confuse objectives with tasks. Objectives are high-level, large, and measurable strategic goals that you set for yourself or your business with the intention of reaching that goal within a set time.

Strategy is about developing plans, projects, and programs, designed to achieve your vision and mission. Determine the success of your strategy by setting measurable objectives or goals.

Tasks are the many actions steps that are necessary to realize the objective. We will examine tasks in more detail in Chapter 9.

Objectives are the milestones of successful strategies.
Set your objectives first.

Tasks are the stepping-stones to meeting your objectives.
Your strategy and objectives determine your tasks.

Jumping into tasks before you are clear about your strategy and the objectives that will measure the success or failure of your strategy is a recipe for burnout. Without a strategy, you will eventually find yourself unfocused, overwhelmed, and overworked.

So … right now, I want you to let go of your action-item task list. If your head is swimming with things to do, take a moment now to empty all those chaotic thoughts and "shoulds" into one place. A mind map (see the tools in the workbook) is a good place to record all the to-do items you have cluttering your mind. Do not worry—the effort to capture and record all the self-imposed demands that are making you anxious has its rewards. Once you capture your to-do list on paper, it will help you recognize your big picture strategy.

If you resonate with the concept of creative tension as discussed in Chapter 2, you can use creative tension to sort out your tasks from your objectives and strategies. You can find an exercise to help you maximize the potential for creative tension inherent in this assignment in the workbook.

Once you have captured all the many tasks you feel you must address, let go of any sense of urgency you may have about getting to the action. Instead, take some time out for leadership. In this case, your leadership task is planning.

Planning for Success

Take a look at all the tasks you have listed. If you completed them all, what would you have? More clients? Higher profits? More impact on the problem you are trying to solve?

Can you see an overall strategy? (Figure 6.2) Given the mission statement you developed in the last chapter, is this strategy likely to bring you the most success?

Google's challenge was to maximize the value of the data they collected while also providing their product free of charge. Their strategy was to market to advertisers and make money through the keyword bid process.

What are the challenges you face as you create your business vision? What strategy do you need in order to overcome those challenges?

My business us a	(Process)
in which	(Transformation)
for	(Stakeholders)

Figure 6.2 Focus your business strategy

Consider these areas for setting strategic objectives (Figure 6.3):

Opportunities	Focus on...
Position:	Become known as...
Clients:	Attract clients that need...
Products and service:	Our core products and services are...
Systems:	Create business systems that will...
Revenue:	Generate revenues of....
Partnerships:	Use partnerships to...
Development:	Create these products....

Figure 6.3 Set strategic objectives

Write down all of the possible strategies you are considering:

WRITE IT DOWN

Given Your Strategy, What's Next?

What Do You Intend to Achieve in the Next 12 Months?

In order to implement your strategy, you need to set specific objectives designed to meet specific milestones. "Milestone" is a term from project management. Milestones mark the point where a project transitions from one phase to another.

Determine Your Milestones

Based on the strategy you have chosen, what milestones do you need reach? What has to happen in the real world in order for your business vision to become a reality? What transitions will accomplish that?

Begin With the End in Mind: Identifying Your Start Up Milestones

Refer back to your vision and mission as described on your Simple Business Plan. Make sure it is clear in your own mind, and then begin to work backward. In order to build the company you imagine by using the strategy you have chosen, what must happen along the way? Your milestones will be *your* milestones, and they will depend on where you are in the overall process. For some entrepreneurs, just completing the exercises in this book will be a milestone. For others, a milestone may be earning $100 or $100K every day.

Start where you are and keep your goals challenging but achievable.

Here are some possible ideas to start the milestone brainstorming process. Using this list and the work you have already done to visualize your business, add more milestones that are unique to your business and its eventual success:

- Product launch
- Doors open
- First revenue
- First key employee
- Specific revenue targets
- Profitability
- Daily income

Your milestones need to be clear, so provide the following details for each event (Figure 6.4):

- Name
- Due Date
- Budget
- Responsible Party

WRITE IT DOWN

Milestone	Due date	Responsible party
Doors open	July 1st	Anne and Scott
First revenue	Sept 30	Anne
First revenue target	Jan 1	Anne
Additional employee	April 30	Anne

Figure 6.4 Determine your milestones

> *Think of starting a business or making money as having sex, just enjoy the process.*
>
> —Naveen Jain

Your Objective Is to Reach Your Milestones

Having clear, prioritized milestones will help you structure your time in order to make steady progress toward your objectives and avoid being distracted by "shiny objects" that have nothing to do with realizing your business goals.

Objectives bring your business planning out of the realm of concepts and ideas and into the real world of clearly defined targets. By applying the principles of SMART goal-setting and being very clear about what needs to happen for your success to become a reality, you will begin to sort through all the clutter and turn it into clear business goals.

Knowing exactly what needs to happen to make your business a success defines the difference between a business *owner* and a business *leader*. You need to embrace the role of business *leader* if you want your business to become a sustainable entity.

Every journey begins with just one step, so begin *your* journey by breaking your audacious and optimistic intentions down into manageable bites. Your goal may be to run a huge international corporation, but you need to pass some attainable milestones along the way. This is particularly true if you are just starting your entrepreneurial journey. What are the objectives you need to accomplish to create and run that international corporation you are imagining? What are the milestones along the way?

Before we move on to reveal the secret of the universal, most important, everybody-needs-this Objective #1, I would like to say a bit more about the importance of SMART goals. Objectives are nothing more than specific goals that will motivate you into action every day of the week. The more Specific, Measurable, Attainable, Relevant, and Time-bound (SMART) your goals are, the better your chances of success will be.

If you are not familiar with SMART, a powerful acronym for goal-setting, I encourage you to read the instructions in the workbook. If you learned about SMART goal-setting in school or in a personal development class, you may still want to review the specifics of the system. I find that most people are positively motivated when they complete the SMART process with their current goals and objectives.

What Do You Need to Survive: Your Cash Flow Objectives?

Do you know what is the most important, everybody-needs-this, number one business objective in all the world?

Survival.

Survival should be your #1 Objective.

To know what you must do in order to survive, begin with the numbers on your Current Reality Analysis. Without an income sufficient to meet the leader's (that's you!) basic needs, the mission will fail. What is the monthly income you need to accomplish your personal survival? What do you need to have in place to realize a consistent income level?

This number, the number you need to live, is measured in cash. You must have sufficient cash flow over and above the expenses of your business each month in order to pay your rent, feed your children, and keep fuel in your car. Late-paying clients can spell real pain and potential failure for a small business owner. You *must* have the cash flow necessary to pay your business expenses as well as your personal needs each month.

To set meaningful cash flow objectives, you first need to determine your cash flow possibilities through a business process called Revenue Modeling. When you do this powerful exercise, you will gain a clear understanding of the potential numbers behind your business model.

Knowing your numbers is essential to knowing your business objectives. In its simplest form, Revenue Modeling is about knowing how many widgets you need to sell in order to make enough money to accomplish your goals.

I find this to be an *extremely* important exercise. Once business builders become clear on what it will take to generate the gross revenue they require, and once they can estimate (with some degree of accuracy) how much of the gross will be taken by monthly expenses, real and measurable sales objectives become very clear.

How to Complete a Revenue Model

In its simplest form, a revenue model answers the question, "Where is the money coming from?" It is a written projection of the potential money to be made on each product and service you sell. As you are starting out, you will use the information from your Current Reality Analysis as well as your cash flow objectives in order to set specific revenue objectives. By working backwards from your revenue objectives, you can determine exactly how many of each product you will need to sell each month in order for your business to survive and thrive.

Step One

Gather all your data including your Current Reality Analysis with your personal cash flow requirements. You will also need an understanding of your projected business expenses.

Consider these categories (Figure 6.5) and determine which of the items are necessary for the success of your business. Estimate your monthly expenses in each category. You may not yet know exactly which of these categories will be part of your strategy, and if this is the case, estimate the expenses you know you will have such as Internet, telephone,

--- Advertising	--- CPA	--- Shipping	--- Travel
--- Marketing	--- Labor	--- Postage	--- Hotel
--- Web design	--- Business fees	--- Computer hardware	--- Flights
--- Internet access	--- Auto expenses	--- Printing/Copying	--- Meals
--- Banking fees	--- Insurance	--- Office supplies	--- Mileage
--- Merchant account	--- Prof. Development	--- Telephone	--- Car rental
--- Computer support	--- Photography	--- Office equipment	--- Transportation
--- Legal	--- Stationery	--- Software	--- Taxes

Figure 6.5 Possible monthly business expenses

labor costs, and so on. You can return to this tool with numbers that are more precise once you have completed your strategic planning.

For a spreadsheet to help with the calculations, see my website.

Step Two

Determine your product offerings. In order to determine your expected revenue, you need to know exactly what you are selling and at what price. Make sure you include all of your streams of income on your list.

Step Three

Choose a desired monthly revenue number. This number should:

- Support your current or desired lifestyle.
- Contribute toward closing any gaps between your current lifestyle and your current income.
- Build trusting professional relationships by covering your business expenses each month.
- Move you steadily toward ever-increasing profits.

The best way to choose this number is to play with the Revenue Model Spreadsheet. Remember, you are looking for a monthly revenue number that is challenging but also do-able. (Figure 6.6)

Step Four

Determine how many of each product you need to sell each month in order to reach your chosen revenue number.

Product	Price	Number sold	
Widget #1	$1	10	$10
Widget #2	$10	4	$40
Widget #3	$20	2	$40
Monthly total		16	$90

Figure 6.6 Determine your revenue goals

I cannot emphasize enough how important it is that you understand your business as a revenue-generating system. If you skip the revenue modeling work, you will never truly understand your business.

You will find a robust revenue modeling spreadsheet on the website that can help you make powerful determinations about your goals and objectives for your business. If you prefer, you can do all the projections on paper with a pencil and perhaps a calculator, but you will gain a deeper understanding of the value of the tool if you also view the videos on my website.

Of all the self-coaching and business start-up tools I offer, the financial revenue modeling spreadsheet is the one most likely to generate powerful insights about your business and its potential for greatness.

Once you have completed the revenue modeling exercise, write down your SMART Revenue Objectives here:

WRITE IT DOWN

Sales and Marketing

This focus on revenue brings us to the nuts and bolts of your business—sales and marketing. Based on your revenue goals, you should have the information you need to set powerful and specific sales and marketing goals.

Sales are the lifeblood of your business. You must have sales goals in order to meet your revenue goals. A sale—which is the moment your warm lead commits to your product—is a product of your marketing. You must attract the attention of the people in your niche, interest them in your product, invite them to enter into a deeper discussion, and actually close the sale. This entire process is easier said than done. Only some of the people you talk to will eventually complete your sales process and purchase something from you. If you want to drive consistent sales, you must maintain an effective and consistent marketing effort. For your business to succeed, you will need both sales and marketing objectives.

Sales Objectives

Do not worry about the sales *process* just yet. For now, focus on your sales goals. Based on the revenue numbers you developed using the Revenue Model Spreadsheet, what are your objectives for sales?

To break the objectives down into goals that are progressively more attainable. Ask yourself:

- What are my sales goals for the year?
- What are my sales goals for the month?
- What are my sales goals for each week?

State your objectives in SMART terms: **S**pecific, **M**easurable, **A**ttainable, **R**elevant, and **T**ime-bound.

Detail your SMART sales objectives here:

WRITE IT DOWN

Marketing Objectives

How many people do you need to speak to each year/month/week in order to close your required number of sales? When you are just starting out, you will have to guess at this number. For the purpose of this step in the process, it is safe to assume you will only close about 20 percent of your encounters.

You will need strategies for attracting the attention of the people you hope to serve and specific objectives for your sales process. Your sales and marketing systems will include specific tasks. We will discuss tasks in Chapter 9. For now, it is enough just to attach approximate real numbers to your baseline requirements.

Detail your SMART marketing objectives here:

WRITE IT DOWN

Beyond Survival

Once you can state clear and measurable objectives for revenue, sales, and marketing, consider setting clear intentions in the following additional areas:

Profit

Your ultimate goal is to have steady, ever-growing, and predictable monthly revenue. Increasing this number beyond expenses is how a business becomes profitable.

You will learn a great deal from completing the business expenses section of the revenue model. When you know exactly what bills to expect and how many widgets you must sell and in what quantities to pay your bills, you will be able to make informed decisions about the day-to-day work required to meet and then exceed your revenue targets.

Determine a revenue goal that exceeds your baseline goal. Make sure it is audacious but achievable.

WRITE IT DOWN

Productivity

One of my very first businesses was making dried flower arrangements. I grew most of the necessary materials in my own garden, dried the flowers in my garage, and assembled the arrangements at the workbench in my basement. Because I enjoyed the production process, I did not pay much attention to my costs in terms of time and materials. When I finally took the time to analyze my costs of production, I found that I was spending far more than I was making. What I actually had was a hobby—not a sustainable business.

The basic formula for estimating productivity includes the effort to produce each item, including time and labor, factored into the selling price.

I made a basic mistake in that my business could not grow because each product was labor intensive and my time to produce was limited. I could not lower my costs because I could not produce enough to buy in bulk or expand my market. In essence, I had a bad business model.

What are your production challenges? Realistically, can you make a profit? In order to calculate your true costs, you need to measure accurately the time and labor needed to create your valuable transformation.

Once you have determined your break-even point, you can then set objectives to increase productivity by hiring additional labor or upgrading your equipment.

List your SMART productivity objectives:

WRITE IT DOWN

Business Ownership Versus Business Leadership

If you have successfully determined concrete goals for the near future of your business, you have moved beyond business ownership to entrepreneurship.

The goals and intentions for your business are no longer merely wishful or theoretical. You are now ready to create and communicate a clear statement of what must happen in the real world in order for your business to meet your expectations. Welcome to business leadership!

Next Steps

In the next chapter, we will address the big question of how, given the gaps between your current reality and your cash flow needs, you can find the money to begin.

Module 6 Workbook—Owning Your Business

Learning Objectives

- Use critical thinking to recognize the strengths in your business model.
- Use the Revenue Model Spreadsheet to set specific sales goals.
- Develop clear strategic goals to meet your revenue model objectives.
- Complete the strategy and objective portion of the Simple Business Plan.

As the leader of your business, you need to know your strengths, how you plan to use those strengths to succeed, and exactly what you must do in order to realize your clear intentions. The tools and exercises here, particularly the *Revenue Modeling Spreadsheet,* will provide you with the information you need.

Exercise	The unique strengths of your business (Left brain)
Exercise	The unique traits of your business (Right brain)
Exercise	Ideation: a creative exercise
Tool	Business challenge checklist
Exercise	Using creative tension
Exercise	S.M.A.R.T goals
Tool	The revenue model

Index to Exercises

Finding the Unique Strengths of Your Business (Left Brain)

The left brain is rational, analytical, and concrete. If this describes your strengths, choose the left brain version of this exercise.

If you are more comfortable working in more emotional and artistic realms you may choose to begin with the following right brain exercise.

Recognize the Unique Traits of Your Business (Right Brain)

Take time to think creatively and then write down your answers to the following questions:

WRITE IT DOWN

We are the best/first/only company to offer—**LIST** the features of your product that either meet a need or solve a problem for your market.

Questions to ask for EACH feature:

- Why should I care about this feature?
- Why did I create this feature?
- Why is the feature important?
- Why is the feature necessary?
- Why doesn't the competition have this feature?
- Why should I care about this feature?

Review your answers and choose one or two features you believe will be most attractive to your market.

WRITE IT DOWN

Rewrite each feature to make the benefits *overt, bold, and brash.* To make each benefit overt add directness, bluntness, and specifics.

- State the overall *benefits* to your customer. Be specific, be obvious, and be direct. What is in it for your customer?
- State the real reason they should believe your claims. How will you deliver on the promises you made?
- State the dramatic difference. How will your product change the world?

Now list any insights you have about the unique value of your product or business.

Do not limit yourself to unique features.

There was once an American beer brewery that set itself apart by claiming the water they used to brew their beer was unique. All beer breweries use water. Water is not necessarily a unique feature. In this case the brewery claimed their water was "pure, mountain spring, water."

Do not limit yourself. List all the features.

Finding the Unique Strengths of Your Business (Right Brain)

This self-coaching exercise addresses your unique values and point of view.

If you are more comfortable working in more rational and analytic realms you may choose to begin with *Recognize the Unique Strengths of Your Business (Left Brain)*. Take time to think and then write down your answers to the following questions:

List the attitudes, ingredients and dimensions that define *why* you choose to create this particular business. Focus on what your business has to offer and how you deliver it.

- What are the differences between your business and the competition?
- Why did you choose this business in the first place?'
- What injustice or problem do you address with your business?
- What are you most proud of regarding your company offers?
- What would your most loyal customers say about what you offer?

Now list the unique traits of your business.

WRITE IT DOWN

Ideation

Ideation is a *process* of forming and relating ideas. Your experience, values and skills are all fodder for new ideas.

Ideation: Let Us Get Creative!

Take one of the business strengths you identified in the previous exercises or a challenge you are concerned about and:

Redefine the Issue

How are you and your target market currently defining the issue? Remember how your mind works? The way you currently define the issue will limit the insights you are able to come up with. When you redefine the issue you will create different definitions and consequently different solutions. (Figure 6.7)

How do we *Attract*	*Customers*	For our *products*
Find	Business owner	Coaching
Communicate with	Managers	Teaching
Engage	Network marketers	Books
Meet with	Bankers	Games
Add to list	Enterprise developers	Workshops
Gain attention	Venture capitalist	Tele seminars
Make friends with	NGOs	Workbooks
Meet	Gov't agencies	CDs
Refer	New ventures	Lectures
Partner with	CEO's	Performances

Figure 6.7 The ideation process

Step One

Start with an opportunity/problem statement that addresses an issue in your target market. For example:

How could we attract more customers able to pay higher prices for our products?

Step Two

Write this creative challenge down on paper or, if you are working in a group, on a flip chart.

Step Three

Pick three of the most interesting words in the sentence and generate creative alternatives (8 to 10) for each word choice. Think of choosing words that represent a simple question: who, when, what, where, and/ or how.

How could we attract more customers able to pay higher prices for our products?

I am a business coach providing guidance and mentoring to emerging entrepreneurs. An ongoing challenge in my business is that my ideal customers do not have (or believe they do not have) resources: time, money, available mental capacity to work with a coach on a regular basis. Given this issue, here is how I might complete this step.

Step Four

Redefine the opportunity by randomly combining words from each of the three categories to create an entirely new opportunity statement:

- How could we ... find venture capitalist for our lectures?
- How could we ... meet with bankers for our coaching?
- How could we ... gain the attention of CEO's for our workshops?

Now take an open-minded, creative look at your possible sentences and see what new ideas you can come up with for a unique product or service to meet the needs of your target market and separate you from the competition.

Do not rush this exercise.

- Allow time for reflection and incubation.
- Creativity requires time.
- Encourage results, inputs, or ideas of any kind.
- Remember: Everything is out there; it has to do with managing one's attention.

Business Challenge Checklist

If you are not exactly sure what areas you may need to work on to improve your chances of business success, try this exercise. (Figure 6.8) To *download a copy* visit the website.

Using Creative Tension to Identify Strategy

If you are caught up in the excitement and potential of your fabulous business vision, you may be feeling some serious creative tension. You can see where you want to go but you cannot (yet) see the path to get there. This can seem like a problem.

A problem with something you care about as much as you care about your business can cause anxiety. If you let your anxiety take hold of your thinking, you will begin to feel stress and, if you are stressed, you will not be doing your best thinking. That is unless, of course, you use what you have learned so far about creative tension to tap into the power of that tension.

If you want to use creative tension to create your vision, do this:

Clearly articulate your vision in as much detail as you can.
This is exactly the vision you have clarified and recorded in your simple business plan and your rich picture. Review it.
Ask yourself: How will I know when I have it?
Notice this question is about outcomes not tasks. If you find your "knowing" is not specific and measurable, ask yourself how someone else will know you have it. For instance, how would I know you had

YES	NO	BUSINESS PLANNING	YES	NO	BUSINESS CREATION
		I have clear goals for my business			I need help with starting a new business
		I know my current reality in relation to my goals			I need help with buying a business
		My business rewards me personally			I need specific industry knowledge
		I have a strategic and tactical plan			I need help identifying my strengths and abilities
		I work my plan every day			I need help leading my business
		I measure my success against clearly defined expectations			I need help in meeting my goals
YES	NO	BUSINESS MODEL	YES	NO	LEAD GENERATION
		I can clearly state the value my product delivers			I know who my customer is
		My price is competitive and acceptable to my buyers			I know what my customer wants
		My cost are known and within targets			I know where to find my ideal customer
		I am aware of common barriers to adoption			I regularly reach out to new customers
					I have a system for keeping in touch with leads
					I have a process for keeping in touch with leads

(Continued)

YES	NO	SALES CONVERSION
		I am comfortable selling
		I believe I solve my customers problems
		I easily and sincerely overcome objections
		I have a useful sales technique
		I successfully close most sales conversations

YES	NO	BUSINESS LEADERSHIP
		I have a business culture built around my business
		I am committed to a larger vision
		I can communicate my vision
		Others believe in my vision

YES	NO	CUSTOMER RETENTION
		I build a relationship with my customers
		My customers continue to do business with me
		My customers recommend my product to others
		I have a strategic product plan
		I measure customer satisfaction

YES	NO	SYSTEMS AND PROCESSES
		I am able to step away from my business
		My processes are documented
		I have an exit strategy
		My business value

Figure 6.8 Business challenge checklist

achieved your vision? This technique takes your intention out of the subjective into the objective world.

Observe your current reality.

You have this information available to you. Review your current reality analysis, your life priorities, your skills inventory, your lifestyle choices. In short, review the structure of your life.

When you have completed this review you will be prepared to notice what next obvious steps come to mind to bridge the gap between your current reality and your vision.

Write your next obvious steps down in no particular order.

Just get it out of your head and onto paper.

WRITE IT DOWN

How SMART Are Your Goals?

This is a well-used tool for forming useful goals and objectives. Many students and workplace teams have been taught this tool at one time or another. Using it is far more effective than just knowing it. Take a look at the objectives you wrote down in Chapter 6 and assess them against the following criteria:

Is It Specific?

Vague goals are a way to avoid failure; or a way to keep from actually having to do anything.

Is It Measurable?

Measure what can be measured and make measurable what cannot be measured.

—Galileo Galilei

The purpose of establishing a measurement is to provide feedback about your results. Without a quantifiable measurement, how will you know what you have actually accomplished? Imagine deciding to lose weight without a measurement. It may be pounds or kilos lost, it may be the way your clothes fit, or it might be your level of comfort in an airplane seat. Each is a measurement, a way to tell if a difference exists. In addition, knowing what you intend to measure will establish clear expectations and strategies about the improvements you intend to make.

Is It Attainable?

People rise and fall to meet your level of expectations.

—John C. Maxwell

The "A" in this acronym can be many different things. I find it is most useful as a way to position your goal somewhere between feet on the ground and head in the sky. Set your vision and measurement to be both attainable and challenging. Challenge yourself with goals that keep you motivated, focused, alert and excited but are achievable.

If you can imagine it, you can achieve it; if you can dream it, you can become it.

—William Arthur War

Relevant/Realistic/Responsible

The R in SMART also has several reference points, including relevant, realistic and responsible.

Is It Relevant?

Every word in this book is about making your business relevant to your life.

Is It Realistic?

You make your goal real when you make your goal attainable. Is it realistic given your current time and resources?

Is It Responsible?

It is also important to know who is responsible. Is it a goal you are responsible for achieving, not someone else.

Much of entrepreneurship and business building is about successfully confronting challenges. If there are obstacles between you and your ultimate dream, set your goals to overcome your most immediate challenge. Hold yourself responsible for your success.

Is It Time Bound?

Setting a deadline is a way to measure and evaluate your results. A firm deadline also creates a sense of urgency. If you fail to meet the time frame you established, then you have an opportunity to reevaluate and reassess. If your goal is not met, do not beat yourself up, instead stop and think; determine why your goal was not achieved.

When you have high but not impossible expectations of yourself, you will achieve more.

It is true that you can have whatever you can imagine but you must pursue it. You must work at it. You must start down a path toward your ultimate goal while setting attainable goals along the way. Unattainable goals are de-motivating, unrealistic, and will set you up for failure which in turn will lower your expectations for success.

The purpose of setting a SMART goal is to achieve it. Remember, as an emerging entrepreneur you are your business. Right now you are setting expectations for yourself, not your future employees, your customers, or your loved ones. The goals you set for your business are goals you must manage. You may engage others, experts in other areas, to help but you are the leader, the manager; you are creating the outcomes. Reread you goal. Are you the actor?

Creating specific, measurable, and reasonably challenging goals is way to demand excellence from yourself.

How to Revenue Model

Learning to use this tool is an important skill.

Believe me. You will have a hard time convincing a bank, an investor, or anyone that you are a serious entrepreneur, if you cannot produce your financials quickly and explain them easily.

The Revenue Model can seem a bit intimidating at first but once you learn the various parts, you will appreciate its remarkable value. When you master the Revenue Model you will be able to:

- Set measurable and specific sales goals.
- Set measurable and specific marketing goals.
- Recognize business issues as they occur.
- Speak with authority about your intentions and expectations for profitability.
- Understand what is most important for your business to succeed.

What Is a Revenue Model?

A revenue model is a description of how a business will earn income (sales), produce profits (pricing), and grow over time (forecasting). The tool you will find here also calculates your *actual* results monthly, quarterly, and annually, provided you are conscientious about entering the data.

For the emerging business owner, revenue modeling can tell you in clear numbers not only what exactly you need to do each month to cover your personal expenses, but also what you need to clear each month to cover the costs of doing business and make a profit.

Once you know how many widgets you need to sell, you will have a very clear picture of your Commander's intent and your strategies for accomplishing your mission will begin to take shape.

The *Revenue Model Tool* you can access on the website is in the form of an Excel spreadsheet. My thanks to Irene Eraklidis formerly of Live Out Loud.com for the creation of the powerful spreadsheet.

Instructions

The spreadsheet consists of four tools and seven separate tabs.

Following you will find written instructions to help you understand and work with this spreadsheet. To download an interactive spreadsheet, visit the website.

Revenue Model Instructions

Expenses—12 Months

This is an interactive spreadsheet listing many possible business expenses. Many of these expenses will be monthly and ongoing (telephone, Internet, insurance, and so on). It is important to recognize the monthly costs that will come out of your monthly gross revenue as profits will only begin once all your obligations have been met. The spreadsheet allows you to forecast your expected costs in each category and record the actual monthly expenses.

Revenue Modeling Business Expenses

Expenses Summary

When you have reliably recorded your business expenses each month, the expenses summary tab will calculate your forecasted and actual results by quarter and annually. This information will be a valuable resource for making future business decisions.

Business Expenses Summary

Revenue Goals

The information produced by the table on this tab is both exciting and valuable. When you have determined your personal cash flow needs and estimated your cost of doing business, you will have a baseline for your break even. Now using the Revenue Goals table you can begin to dream. What is the revenue you want? What is the revenue you dream of? Enter the figures and you will learn what you have to generate each month and day to turn your vision into reality.

Revenue Model Goal Planning

Revenue Months 1 to 6, Revenue Months 7 to 12

The next two tabs are the working pages where you enter you product list, your pricing, your forecasted sales by month, and your actual sales by month. The information spreads over two tabs only to make it easier to see on one screen; the two tabs together represent an entire year of projections and actual results.

Rev Months 1–6
Rev Months 7–12

Revenue Model 12-Month Summary

When you have completed a year of date entry, you will find on this tab your forecasted and actual revenue results by quarter. With this information you will be able to recognize the need for any change and to re-evaluate your strategy.

12-Month Summary

I hope you can appreciate the amazing power of knowing your numbers and you can appreciate the power of this *Revenue Modeling* tool to help you know your financials on an ongoing basis. If you are still reluctant to drill down into the numbers, go find someone right now who can help you. If you are ready to step into your role as a powerful business leader, begin by downloading the Revenue Model Spreadsheet.

Click here to go to the revenue model download page.

Then, to learn to use this powerful tool, watch these videos:

- *Overview of the Revenue Model Spreadsheet*
- *Revenue Modeling: Business Expenses*
- *Revenue Modeling: The Revenue Goals Tabs*
- *Revenue Modeling: The Revenue Modeling Tabs*

CHAPTER 7

How to Finance Your Brilliant Idea

Your actions are your only true belongings.

—Allan Lokos

The question I get most often from hopeful entrepreneurs is, "Where can I find the money to start my business?"

To me this question shows a lack of creative thinking. A successful entrepreneur needs a bit more initiative and lot more problem-solving skills than evidenced by asking a question such as, "How is it possible to get someone to give me money?"

The more appropriate question should be, "How can I create a business someone would gladly invest in?"

Investors are in the business of using their own money to make more money for themselves. Unless you can convincingly demonstrate a plan for returning more value to the investor than the investor plans to give to you—like gold rolling down hill and jumping into their pocket—they will not give you money.

Banks make money by charging interest on the money they lend (called the principal) and getting that principal plus interest back within the agreed upon timeframe. If they have doubts about your ability to repay the money along with the added interest, they will not lend it. Banks are notorious for their strong aversion to risking their money.

So ... the answer to the question, "How can I get someone to give me money?" is to build a business and prove you have a system that can make money. You will be able to demonstrate your business's ability to make money when you can show you have met clear objectives. You do this by having specific measurements and keeping track. In addition, you will need a robust market, a loyal customer base, and a plan for increasing both. You need to show any potential investors that you can make *more* money than the amount of money they are considering investing in your business.

You must give every man more in value than he gives you in cash value.
—Wallace Wattles

Failure Is Likely but Survivable

So there it is ... the classic Catch 22. In order to have a business that makes enough money to attract investors, you first have to build a business that makes money.

Welcome to the true work of entrepreneurship. The job of an entrepreneur is to confront obstacles with determination and to keep at it until you have figured out a workable solution.

To begin the business creation process, you need money. Nevertheless, for most emerging entrepreneurs this money will be yours—not someone else's. In truth, this focus toward self-reliance is only fair because the initial risk *should* be yours. When you invest your own money, you not only show commitment to your business idea, you also create stronger personal motivation. In the long run, this will actually reduce your risks.

Given the statistics, there is a fair chance your first business might indeed fail. If you have carefully read and worked through this book thus far, your chance of success is far better than average. However, startup failure is still a possibility. What if all your assumptions up to this point are wrong?

Forecasts may tell you a great deal about the forecaster; they tell you nothing about the future.
—Warren Buffett

If you are wrong or if things change (and they will), your business may fail. If your business fails, you (or someone) will lose all of your invested capital, which is all of the money spent on building the business thus far. If this happens and you have not been careful enough in planning, you may find yourself back at square one with no business and no money. You will be on the floor and you will have to pick yourself up, dust yourself off, and start all over again. Only this time you will be determined not to make the same mistakes. This experience will undoubtedly be painful, but you will have the consolation of knowing you are not alone. Business failure is a painful lesson; it is also a common experience among successful entrepreneurs. While startup failure is uncomfortable, it is also survivable. Unless …

… unless you financed the building of your business with loans leaving you with substantial debt. If you owe money to a bank or have an agreement with investors when you fail, you will find yourself not on the floor, but in a deep hole instead. In comparison, it is relatively easy to pick yourself up off the floor. But when you are in a hole, you have to crawl out. And depending on how deep that hole is, it can take you a very long time to surface.

If you are an emerging entrepreneur, consider your first business to be a learning experience. Allow for the possibility that you might make a few valuable mistakes. You can manage your risk by bootstrapping.

Bootstrapping

Bootstrapping is a verb meaning to get oneself out of a challenging situation using existing resources already available. In terms of starting a business, bootstrapping particularly refers to creating a small-scale business that begins with the entrepreneur's own money and relies on customer revenue to continue.

Using your own money is probably the biggest hurdle a new entrepreneur faces. After all, if you had money—lots of money—you might not be as motivated to work hard to succeed in starting your own business.

I understand that money is a challenge, but bootstrapping is still a possibility. In order to bootstrap your startup, you need to cultivate patience, set small, achievable milestones, and work hard to accomplish each one. It may take more time but, in the end, you will have the benefit of keeping all of your profits.

Now is the time to, once again, take inventory of all of your financial assets. You should have this information available if you have completed the Current Reality Analysis task. If you have, you will remember that assets are anything you own that you could sell for cash money. Generally, available self-funding advice often suggests cashing out or borrowing against these assets like home equity, retirement accounts, stocks, and bonds.

This is good advice for older, well-established people who have accumulated significant assets. However, for the young, creative, and less well-heeled person—which includes most people these days—bootstrapping can be a slow process. Do not let that discourage you. Remember entrepreneurship is both a process and a lifestyle. As you maneuver your way to profit, you will not only learn something about creative problem solving, but also you will value the money more and keep more of it for yourself when you have worked hard for it.

Begin by Offering a Service

Manufacturing and retail sales can be expensive businesses to start. Providing a service such as consulting, contracting, or informational products can be comparatively inexpensive to get off the ground. What service can you provide to your market niche that will begin to generate revenue without a large outlay of cash upfront? What strategies and measurement tools do you need to establish in order to track your progress toward your monetary startup goal?

Do Not Quit Your Day Job … Yet

I know this is probably not what you want to hear, but it is wise advice. By maintaining your life with a steady source of income while you build your business, you will insure your ability to continue building your business despite the inevitable setbacks and frustrations you will discover along the way. For entrepreneurs who want to build lasting systems, minimizing risks by keeping your day job is the slow and steady path to sustainable success.

Cut Costs

If you want to speed up the process of creating a business on the side, cut costs wherever you can. While your day job is meant to pay the bills, the fewer bills you have, the faster you will make your way to the magic number you need from your finances in order to start your business.

Increase Revenue

A famous American business mentor advocates giving up one's daily designer coffee (at a cost of $3 to $4 each) to save money for starting a business. Another mentor of mine scoffs at this idea and says, "Do not give up anything! Just go make money."

Cutting costs or increasing revenue—which one works for you?

Can you sell something? In tech companies, this is called rapid prototyping, meaning you create a product quickly and begin selling it as soon as possible. This starts the money flowing, and similar to priming a water pump, more money will follow faster and faster.

One young client of mine has a vision to build an empire, he is gathering his startup cash by making and selling his own hip-hop CDs. His idea has a low cost to entry, which makes it a great bootstrapping idea with the added bonus of being a good way to hone his sales skills.

Can your expenses be cut? Look again at your Current Reality Analysis. Do you see expenses that are nice to have but not necessary? Entertainment, alcohol, travel, and clothing?

Or can you do both—increase revenue and decrease expenses? This simple formula is often the answer to finding more cash. It is a workable formula and similar to the proverbial "eat less and exercise more" formula for losing weight.

When You Are Ready to Borrow

Bootstrapping is a reasonable way to learn the ropes, test your idea, and prove your worth. Once you have done that and you are ready to expand, you can move forward by considering different options for obtaining the capital you need for your startup.

8.4% of the adult population in the world commands 83.3% of global wealth while almost 70% possess only 3%.
—International Conference on Population and Development
(ICPD) Beyond 2014 Report

Venture Capital

Investors are not in the business of bank rolling dreams; they intend to make money. An investor in your venture will want to see a certain level of expertise and familiarity with your market. They will want to see proof that your idea will work, and they will want to know when they will receive a return on their investment. This is usually a point in the future when the company will either be sold or go public. If your business is not at this level of stability yet, venture capital is not for you.

However, if venture capital is your goal, you need to be diligent about the measurements you set in the previous chapter. An accurate and verifiable Revenue Model Spreadsheet showing a history of ever-increasing sales and profits is a powerful argument in your favor. Your success at "making your numbers" will be the data you need to attract the money you want.

Angel Investors

Angel investors are not really angels, but they are investors. In return for an individual "angel" investing in your company, you must give that individual a percentage of ownership in your company—usually forever. Angel investors do not typically make large investments, so their percentage of ownership may not be large. However, angel investors are often interested in having a say in how the company operates. You, as the emerging entrepreneur and owner of the startup, may benefit from the expertise of an angel investor ... or not. Vet your investor with as much diligence as he or she is vetting you, and then proceed with caution.

Conventional Bank Loans

Banks do not like risks. Banks will always want to know that the money they loan you will be paid back exactly as the terms were spelled out in the agreement. Proving your credit worthiness to a bank can be difficult, time consuming, and frustrating. Even so, at some point, you will want the credibility of a solid credit score, so you should start building your credit now—you will be glad you did.

If you intend to be a lifelong entrepreneur, developing a relationship with a banker is a valuable asset. Banks may be conservative, but they are in the business of lending money. If and when you have established your credentials as an entrepreneur, a supportive banker might be your best friend—at least in the business world.

Credit Card Loans

Credit card loans have restrictive terms and incredibly high interest rates. Choosing this method of start-up financing requires careful management and a high degree of risk tolerance. If you intend to choose this method of financing, find a card with a low interest rate, watch your account carefully, do not miss a payment, and plan to transfer balances as soon as possible to maintain the low interest rate.

Government Grants

A grant is an award of funds, usually from an organization, for a specific purpose, and typically, grants do not have to be repaid. Governments, charitable organizations, arts foundations, and nonprofit organizations are all potential grant sources.

A good place to discover available grants and apply for them as well is on the Internet. You can search for certain phrases such as government grants, public charities, or private foundations, and so on, and it will result in a list of possibilities to check. Make sure to read the grant guidelines carefully because organizations give money away based on what matters to *them*—not what matters to you. If your business plan doesn't match the organization's mission, it is a waste of time to apply.

> *Thou shalt not forget that money is only money and not character or fame.*
>
> —Steven J. Lee

Accelerators and Incubators

Incubators and accelerators help firms grow by providing guidance and mentorship.

Incubators work with emerging businesses by providing business skills training and access to financing and professional networks.

The focus of a business accelerator is on rapid growth in order to move a business beyond the startup phase. The resources available from an accelerator program can help a business builder sort out organizational, operational, and strategic difficulties they might be facing with their business.

The value exchange is different for every service provider, so to explore the possibilities in your area, begin with an Internet search that includes your location as a factor of the search.

Crowd-Funding

One interesting possible source of resources is crowd-funding. This is a term used to describe raising money through the collective effort of various individuals. Crowd-funding is usually organized via the Internet—but not always. Whom do you know that might be willing to invest a small amount of money in order to have access to a service or product you intend to provide? Whom do you know who might invest in your start-up just because they love you and want to see you succeed? How can you reach out to these people, and what can you offer them in return for their support?

Just like your business, business financing is a profit-making enterprise and anyone who offers you money will expect something in return. If you can build a profitable business on your own by using your own resources, you will not only maintain control, you will also keep all the profits. Another great aspect of doing it with your own resources is the boost it will give you in terms of establishing your credibility as an accomplished entrepreneur faster. You will be seen as someone who has acquired valuable skills and experience, and someone with the ability to start another successful business using OPM—other people's money.

Next Steps

Congratulations. You have done most of the hard work of business planning. You have all the information you need to complete the vision, mission, strategy, and objectives portion of the simple business plan. If you have not already, take time now to write down the results of all your thinking up to this point.

In the next chapter, we will tackle the details of business building: measuring results to inform your actions. I know you are waiting to get into action so let's go.

Module 7 Workbook—How to Finance Your Brilliant Idea

Learning Objectives

- Understand the difference between various financing options.
- Develop a financial plan for reducing personal debt (optional).
- Develop a financial needs assessment.
- Develop a plan for financing your business vision.

Money won't create success, the freedom to make it will.

—Nelson Mandela

There is no magic to acquiring capital for your business. If you lack the resources you need to begin building your dream, begin at the beginning. Acknowledge the real numbers of your current reality and create a strategy for generating the money you need to begin. Use that seed money to make more money. That is how entrepreneurs do it.

Information	How to establish credit
Information	How to pay off debt
Activity	Confronting financial need
Activity	Create your financial plan

Index to Exercises

How to Establish Personal Credit

I often receive e-mails similar to this one:

I am 22 years old. I am a young man with a vision, ambition, passion, plans, and big dreams and I have a positive mindset. I've read your profile and it got me interested. My inner voice tells me that you are the right person that will help me through my

situation and to help me achieve my goal and turn my dream to
the reality of owning a global company. Let us get straight to the
point about why I am writing this e-mail. I have a dream, a vision,
and an idea that will impact the world. I dream of owning one of
the biggest companies in the world.

I admire and envy this young man's exciting vision. I would like to
help him, but chances are he will not like my advice. To a young person
seeking to build one of the biggest companies in the world I would say:

Begin a banking relationship by opening a checking and savings
account. You may be able to get your first credit card through your
bank.

Pay your utility bills in full and on time. If your household utilities
are not in your name, consider taking over a least one account.

Be steady and consistent. When applying for credit or a loan, be able
to show a history of employment and a steady home address.

Apply for a department store or gas credit card. Get started building
your history by *charging only the amount you can afford to pay off
every month.*

Manage your credit wisely for six months and then get more. To
establish a well-rounded credit history, diversify your loan types:
credit card, auto loan, and student loan.

Good credit is essential to establishing your credibility as a stand-up
business person. If you cannot manage your personal financial situation
with professionalism and honor, how will you manage your business
finances? More importantly, if your finances are in ruins, why would anyone trust you with their money?

How to Pay Off Your Debts

Commitment:

- *Definition #1: The state or quality of being dedicated to a cause,
  activity, and so on.*

- *Definition #2: An engagement or obligation that restricts freedom of action.*

Finding oneself in consumer debt with credit cards, school loans, car loans, is a common problem for many people. Realizing the extent of the money one owes is often an emotional outcome of completing the *Current Reality Analysis* exercise.

Consumer debt is a hard rock but one that must be moved; there is no way around it. So if you find your payments on your monthly bills restricts your freedom to act, commit to following this plan until you find your way clear to saving the money you need to build your dream.

Step One

Find some extra money.

I know, I know. But if you keep doing the same thing over and over, what will change? Come on. You can do it. If this seems impossible, you may want to consider coaching around this issue.

Try this:

Consider liquidating any big-ticket items that you bought on time. Track your spending. Keep all receipts and analyze your spending every month. Look for small things that add up: books, music, buying lunch at the office, beer or wine. Bite the bullet. What small luxury can you forego just until your credit is reestablished?

Step Two

Establish a specific amount you will commit to paying toward your debt each month.

Do this:

Gather all your credit card statements. Find the card with the highest interest rate. Add the extra money you have found to the minimum payment for this card. Do this until this card is paid off. Got it?

You will pay the minimum payment plus the added amount each month by the due date.

Each month continue to pay the minimum amount on all your other cards by the due date. When the first card is paid off, add the extra money *plus* the minimum payment you were paying on the now-retired debt to the card with the next highest interest rate. Continue until this card is paid off.

You will continue rolling this extra money and each of the minimum payments amounts for each retired debt into the next card payment until you are debt free. When all your cards show a zero balance, celebrate. Pay cash for this celebration. Start rebuilding your credit.

Other Things You Can Try

Talk to Your Creditors

- Negotiate. Accept the fact you will have to give something up. In every business transaction there must be a value exchange. See what you can work out.
- Shop around for lower interest rate cards and transfer your balances. This is a practice that benefits you more than the credit card companies so be sure to do your due diligence.
- Pay attention to how long the introductory rate lasts.
- Be aware of any transfer fee.
- Do not be willy-nilly. Read the fine print. Calculate the pay-back. Make sure *you* benefit financially from this move.

Creating Your Financial Plan

Startup Costs

What will you need to begin your business? Consider everything from your business license, furnishings, equipment, marketing materials, even the catering for your grand opening party. You may want to review your rich picture of your business to help you with your thinking.

Regular Monthly Expenses

You have already captured these in your Revenue Modeling worksheet.

Assumptions

No doubt you have found you need to make assumptions in order to estimate your future expenses. Write down those assumptions now.

You will find this information useful when you revisit your forecast in a few months.

Goals

Once you have a clear estimate of your financial need, you are ready to create SMART financial goals.

WRITE IT DOWN

Confronting Financial Need

The only way around is through.

—Robert Frost

- Make an appointment with a small business banker and present your business plan. Discuss what, if any, changes you would need to make to be eligible for a loan.
- Review your current reality and determine where you can access financial resources to invest in your business.
- Review your revenue model. In what challenging but achievable ways can you increase the revenue from your business?

CHAPTER 8

How to Know if Your Business Is a Success

Your SMART goals and objectives include measurements and your monetary goals include measurements as well. Anyone who is considering supporting your business with an investment will want to know your numbers. To monitor your progress, you need a system for keeping track of your measurements. The Revenue Model is a good place to start, but you also need a plan for moving your "actual number" (your current reality) closer to your forecast or goal number, and a plan for celebrating when you reach each milestone.

No matter the size or intention for your business, you will not succeed—at least not in any sustainable way—until you have put numbers to your success.

What You Know So Far

You know your current financial reality as well as exactly where you are because the numbers on your Current Reality Analysis Worksheet precisely pinpoint your starting place.

You know where you are going—you have a vision, a strategy, and specific objectives. You have the specific numbers that will tell you when you actually arrive at the place of your vision and goals.

Revisiting Creative Tension

If it seems these two numbers—the number of your current reality and the number of your vision—have a very distant relationship to each other, do not despair. Think of the distance between your two numbers as the tension you must have in order to create the business of your dreams.

*There will always be tension in the beginning of the creative pro-
cess, for there will always be a discrepancy between what you want
and what you have. Why? Because creators bring into being creations
that do not yet exist. In fact, part of your job as a creator is to form
this tension.*

—Robert Fitz

Do you remember the rubber band illustration? If the tension is loose, there is no motivation to change. When the rubber band stretches tight, there is motivation to reduce the tension. When you become aware of the tension between your reality and your vision, it becomes easier to reduce the tension than it is to live with it. Your motivation to reduce the tension by creating something new—including new revenue—will activate your creative process.

You already have a clear picture of the system you need to build. You know the results you need to generate in order to create your dream. If there is a gap, all you need to do is get to work. The trick is in knowing *which* work is the most important to do first. As the leader of your business, you need to prioritize the tasks that will move your current reality numbers closer to your vision numbers. You will know what is working by the measurements you choose.

What to Measure

Measure what is important, according to your objectives. What do you need to measure in order to know when you have achieved success according to your objectives? What is the most important thing your business needs to succeed? Is it the number of items sold? The number of names on your list? Partnerships? Cash flow? Contracts signed? Determine what causes money to flow into your business circle. If necessary, break down your objectives to manageable chunks. What do you need to accomplish in the next three months, the next six months, or the next year?

State your goals and accomplishments in measurable terms. Assigning measurements will keep you from developing a to-do list prematurely. Measurements are not about what you need to *do*. Instead, measurements are about what you need to *accomplish*.

Start With Your Revenue Goals

If you have not completed the revenue modeling exercise in Chapter 6, this chapter will be difficult to grasp. You are missing a valuable opportunity if you have not yet downloaded the tool and learned how to use it. Do not let the numbers intimidate you. The Revenue Model Spreadsheet is simply a tool to help you think. You will do the actual thinking, then the tool will complete the technical calculations for you. As a potential business leader, spreadsheets are your friend. If you are not already familiar with how to use spreadsheets, set a professional development objective to become familiar with how a basic spreadsheet program (such as Microsoft Excel) works, or hire someone who does.

The goal-planning worksheet within the Revenue Model Spreadsheet is a powerful way to set your high-level profit objectives.

If you are not comfortable using spreadsheets, try the following simple model (Figure 8.1). This model only requires basic math skills. For a detailed explanation on how to use this spreadsheet, please watch the video on my website.

Revenue model goal planning			
	Minimum	Stretch	Home run
Annual sales goal			
Monthly sales goal		$ -	$ -
Weekly sales goal		$ -	$ -
Daily sales goal			
Assumes five days per week		$ -	$ -

Figure 8.1 Revenue model goal planning

Step 1: Determine your annual income goals. Your income must be enough to cover the expenses of your business while also providing sufficient income for you and your family. This is your minimum annual revenue goal.

Step 2: Set a challenging stretch goal with a number that is exciting and a little scary, yet very possible.

Step 3: (Optional): Choose a goal that seems *almost* impossible, but one that would also be absolutely amazing to achieve.

Step 4: Divide your annual goals by 12 (the number of months in a year). This is your monthly sales goal.

Step 5: Divide your monthly sales goal by four (the number of weeks in a month). This is your weekly sales goal.

Step 6: Divide your weekly sales goal by five (the number of workdays in a week). This is your daily sales goal.

What Will You Do to Meet Your Daily Sales Goals?

Sales and Marketing

As we discussed previously, you need strategies in order to meet your sales goals. You need marketing strategies to find the people you can serve with your business. Once you have found your potential customers, you need sales strategies to help them choose to purchase your solution to their problem or need. As a business leader, it is your job to monitor the results of your strategies and make the necessary creative business decisions to move your current reality numbers closer to the numbers of your business vision.

Your first objective as a business owner is to make money, but there may be additional aspects important to your business that you also need to consider when you are setting your objectives.

Measure Your Objectives

Besides making money, what are the other long-term objectives for your business? Do you want to expand into new markets? Launch a new product? Hire key employees? If so, how can you measure your progress in terms of those objectives?

Measure Performance

It is not enough to merely set measurements and then forget about them. You must monitor performance. In order for your business to succeed, you must hold yourself and your staff accountable for achieving your business objectives. You must be able to adjust your processes as needed in order to improve the results.

For example, suppose you determine that you need to sell a certain number of widgets in May. Your measurements should be able to tell you if you did or did not reach your goal number in sales. If you did not reach that number, you need to improve performance. Note that performance does not always mean human performance. As a business grows more complicated, the root cause of business problems become increasingly more difficult to determine. In order to determine and then fix the source of a business problem, you must first be able to identify accurately the problem. Pinpointing the problem takes numbers. What does it take to sell one widget. How many people must you call? How many e-mails must you send? How many orders must you process? Set a goal and measure the results.

Measure Financials

Keep track of the cash! If you have read this far in the book, you are probably thinking, "Duh!" However, you just might be the exception. I know many emerging business people who do not keep track of their money. Money comes in, money goes out, and their business limps along—sometimes for years—without any real understanding of the balance sheet.

As a young woman, I worked in a small bicycle repair shop owned by a former garbage truck driver. He paid me directly from the cash register without keeping any record of the transaction or payout. He was a generous man and he often bought lunch for the staff using money from the register without keeping a record of the money spent. He even kept his unopened bank statements under the counter.

Although he was a good and generous man, he was a very poor businessperson. Without a record of cash in and cash out, he had no way of knowing if his business was making money or losing money. Eventually, he could no longer find the cash he needed to stay in business. He did not have enough money to pay his rent, pay his suppliers, or even feed his family, so he closed the doors to his business and went back to hauling garbage. Moreover, of course, his business failure left me without a job.

If you are not sure of your fixed and variable expenses, see the business expenses tab of the revenue-modeling tool. Make a goal to record accurately your expenses each and every month.

As your business and assets grow, balance sheets can become complicated. If numbers are not your cup of tea, hire a bookkeeper … soon! Do not allow your important information to accumulate. The numbers—particularly your cash flow numbers—are your personal canary in the coalmine. If your cash flow is not at least equal to (or preferably more than) your expenses, you need to adjust your business practices. Recognizing and resolving the imbalance sooner rather than latter is critical to success.

Measure Time

Most new businesses are not profitable in the beginning. There are startup expenses involved, and there is time needed to ramp up. Knowing how much time and money you are burning in the start-up phase is an extremely valuable measurement.

Your revenue model can help determine your measurements. Your sales forecast and actual sales can indicate where you have to be each month of the year in order for your business to stay afloat.

Measure Growth

Regardless of your initial revenue goals, you have to grow in order to build a sustainable business.

No matter where you are in the business startup process, you need to set goals for acquiring new customers and closing more sales. In order to do this effectively, you need baseline data. Baseline data is a record of your current reality numbers. Your numbers can measure sales per week, new customers, returning customers, expenses, or something else, but choose to measure numbers that represent your objectives and immediately begin to keep track. You cannot be sure you whether or not you have made progress unless you can compare your numbers to the data from where you started.

As a leader, it is your responsibility to understand your numbers and use the information to make decisions. It is not necessarily your role to populate the spreadsheet fields. Data entry and bookkeeping are roles that can and, in many cases, should be assigned to other members of your team. However, it is your responsibility to know what the numbers are, and analyze them in light of your goals and objectives. But it is most important that you recognize your responsibility to make business decisions based on the data and then verify that those decisions are carried out.

Adjust the Tension

If you find you are not reaching your number goals, do not be discouraged—adjust! Adjusting is the work of business leadership. Things change, assumptions can be wrong, and stuff happens. Your responsibility as an entrepreneur and business leader is to be focused on finding solutions.

Remember the tension of the tightly stretched rubber band? Remember how strong the tension was when you had a vision, but you did not have a plan, specific goals, or any idea of how you were really going to get there? By now you have traveled a good distance down the road toward your vision and the tension has decreased—then something happens. Something *always* happens, so do not waste time cursing the gods, fate, your genes, and so on. Instead, see this seemingly negative event as an opportunity to recreate the motivating, challenging, and exciting creative tension that started you down this entrepreneurial path in the first place.

Your measurements tell you when something is keeping you from reaching your objectives in the way you envisioned. If you are keeping the right measurements, you will have a good idea of what that something is. So … what are you going to do about it? Can you create a solution? What else can you try? Who else might help? If this problem were already solved, what would the solution look like? What is the quality of your thinking about this particular obstacle? Ask yourself these and similar questions and craft a new vision. Ratchet up the tension between your current reality and your vision for the future of your business. Tap into your creative side and find a way; that is the magic and fun of entrepreneurship.

> *Any change, even a change for the better, is always accompanied by drawbacks and discomforts.*
>
> —Arnold Bennett

Entrepreneurs who fail to set, review, and adjust their business measurements are the entrepreneurs who do not survive.

Next Steps

Business measurements are often detailed and complex, but when you are just beginning to keep track, keep it simple. Begin with baseline estimates and use them to set up a system to track your real numbers. Be intentional about capturing your data. At least once a quarter review your data, monitor your progress, and adjust accordingly.

Setting measurements is the key to developing a clear and specific to-do list. A clear and specific to-do list is the key to staying focused on your priorities and staying focused on your priorities is the key to managing your successful business.

In the next chapter, we will look at action planning. Now that you know where you are going, you are ready to clarify the tasks you need to do in order to reach your intended destination.

Module 8 Workbook—How to Know When Your Business Is a Success

Learning Objectives

- Demonstrate executive leadership through planning and evaluation.
- Establish performance measures for all critical areas of your business.
- Tie each measurement to important objectives of your business.

Do not get caught up in developing elaborate data collection systems. Keep it as simple as possible. Make sure that the data is collected religiously and that you, as the leader, review the data on a regular basis.

Information	Data collection systems

Index to Exercises

Data Collection

K.I.S.S. Keep It Simple, Stupid

Once you know what information you need to collect to track your progress toward your objectives, you will need to establish a system for collecting data, storing the information, and analyzing the results on a regular basis.

The *Revenue Model Spreadsheet* is a very useful tool for tracking and measuring your actual sales against your projected sales and tracking your actual revenue over time.

What other information do you need to track? Beyond sales and marketing each business will have different strategies and consequently different objectives to pursue. Given your objectives, what is the simplest and easiest way to track your results?

Devise a system that works for you. Choose a system that demands as little time and effort as possible. Data collection and entry is a dull business. If possible, hire someone to do it for you. You are really only interested in the results, not the day-to-day chore of collecting the information. Consider carefully what information you need to collect and how best to monitor and adjust your progress toward your goals.

Begin by Asking These Questions

- Why are you collecting this information? What is the objective this data collection process will measure?
- How will you display the information once it is collected? Work backward from your vision of how the information will be most useful to you.
- What information is required by the presentation tool you will use?
- Where can you find the data you will need?
- What is the easiest and most efficient way to collect this data?
- Who will collect the measurement data needed?
- What information will they collect?
- Where will the data be collected and stored?
- When or at what point in the process will the data be collected?

WRITE IT DOWN

Write down your plan. You will find these written instructions useful when you are ready to train someone else to do the data entry task for you.

CHAPTER 9

Action Planning: How to Do the Right Thing

Let us recap … so far in this book you have:

- Created an Inspiring Vision of Success.
- Identified a Real and Meaningful Service or Solution.
- Developed a Detailed (but simple) Business Plan.
- Established a System to Continually Check Your Progress.

Finally, we get to the place where most entrepreneurs choose to begin—the action.

For most of the emerging entrepreneurs I meet, the action steps involved in building their businesses often become an exercise in chaos. Managing chaos every day has its rewards but, in most cases, the rewards are not monetary, long-lasting, or productive.

No plan survives contact with the enemy.

—Colonel Tom Kolditz

Does the following description fit your life?

On Monday mornings, your to-do list flows over the edge of your desk. A few important items may even fall on the floor, but delegation is not an option. In your business operation, there is only you. Everything needed for your business and dreams depends on you. You know you are missing opportunities each and every day, and you are frustrated by all that unrealized potential. If only you could work harder, longer, and faster, you would realize success.

Many entrepreneurs thrive on the battle-ready excitement of this kind of high-energy existence. Some of them—the lucky ones—even meet with success, but others burn out.

I applaud you for staying with the thinking tasks of leadership we have explored up to this point. With so much real and action-oriented work to do, it may seem like a waste of time and mental energy to merely *think* about your business leadership. After all, if you have no staff, who benefits when you take the time to focus on your goals, renew your vision, and review your strategy?

This is a common objection to the time-consuming task of thinking voiced by hard-working and busy business builders. For these action-oriented entrepreneurs, the position of business leader goes unfilled as they gather the tools of their trade—cell phones, meeting requests, proposals, presentations, and networking—and get to work.

When Action Is Only Action

When action is the only criteria for action, the work week begins as Monday slips into Tuesday. On Tuesday, the entrepreneur's best intentions are blindsided by traffic jams, failures of communications, technical glitches, and customer complaints. Business intentions become clouded. By Wednesday, it is proverbial "firefighting" all day long. On Thursday, it is time to clean up the mess created during the first three days of the week, and then on Friday, if the entrepreneur is lucky, he or she takes a brief pause from the action in order to survey the rubble of the week that is ending.

With such a busy and difficult workweek, it does not take long for the vision and mission of the business to become obscured. Sales numbers, marketing efforts, and even cash flow are neglected and results start to falter.

The problem with getting into action too soon is the actions you choose to take may not be the actions necessary to move the numbers on your revenue model closer to the numbers of your goals. And if you are all action and no leadership, you may not even notice until it is too late.

To move steadily and effectively toward your big picture goals each week, it is important to remember your objectives and strategy. It is your role to ensure that your business objectives are clearly articulated and your carefully established strategies are consistently enacted in every aspect of your business. What follows is a simple, quick-thinking system to consciously acknowledge, review, and refocus your intentions for each aspect of your business every week. It is a system where nothing slips through the cracks to smolder unattended.

How to Be the Chief Executive Officer of Your Business

The role of a CEO is threefold:

Decision Maker: As the final authority in your business, you must make important decisions about strategy, purpose, priorities, and risks. Having a clear strategy is the key to making the best decision possible each time you have a choice.

Leader: A corporate CEO often answers to a board of directors. As a small business owner, you are most often responsible to stakeholders, a group that may include your family, the bank, and your own dreams and desires. As a leader, it is your responsibility to hold true to your vision and the values and goals of your stakeholders.

Manager: A small business has many moving parts. As the leader of your own business, you must manage the day-to-day operations while doing all of the day-to-day work or at least most of it. It is your daily responsibility to focus on the big picture in your mind. You must take time for leadership while taking care of the little tasks that keep your business running on a day-to-day basis.

How to Lead Your Business Every Day

To manage all of these roles effectively as you are working in your business at the same time, you need to take these five things *very* seriously:

- Planning
- Operations
- Finance

- Marketing
- Sales

A big business CEO keeps track of these moving parts by regularly meeting with his chief executive managers in each of these areas. In order for you, the small business owner, to replicate the tactics of the CEO, you must *consciously* focus on each of these areas of your business on a regular basis, at least once a week.

Finding Time to Lead Your Business

I know you want to be busy because being busy feels important and productive. Frankly, busy work is easier and more invigorating than the work of thinking usually is. But by now I hope I have convinced you that thinking about your business, that is, *leading* your business, actually *is* your business. You can accomplish the important leadership thinking needed in just 10 minutes each day—10 minutes. That is all the time you need to carve out of your morning schedule in order to review the important goals for your business and your life. Just 10 minutes each day is all the time that is necessary to monitor your efforts in each of the five important areas of your business.

Let us break it down.

Monday, You Are the "Big Boss"

Before you turn to your e-mail, check your phone messages or send an SMS to confirm your lunch meeting—but not before you have had your morning coffee and/or breakfast because you need to be focused and alert for the task—take 10 minutes to review your business plan, reconnect with your vision, and revisit your priorities.

As the week progresses, you will be meeting (even if it is only in your mind) with the leaders of each area of your business: operations, finance, marketing, and sales. You will do this in order to set action item priorities based on the big picture of who you are, who you serve, and how you want your business to be perceived by the world in general. This creative and motivating vision is the result of the work you have done so far in this book. What you have learned about yourself and your mission in this world is important. Keep it in front of you each week because it can be easily lost to the noise and confusion of business action. In order to reconnect, you need to spend quiet, intentional time on bringing your plan to the forefront of your mind.

On Mondays, take just 10 minutes to review your business plan, remind yourself of your strategies and intentions, and set your priority outcomes for the week.

Tuesday Is Operations Day

The operations of a business include all the moving parts required to ensure your business makes money. Every business, small or otherwise, must stay efficient, effective, and current. This includes everything from keeping your car running to repairing the roof on the warehouse and many frustrating and time-consuming tasks in between.

If you are the sole employee of your business, it is easy to get caught up in these operational tasks. It is a temptation to see each task as urgent and important because, despite the frustration, this type of operational activity is often easy to complete and undemanding when compared to many of the harder aspects of your job.

I once had a client who would regularly drive to a store 40 miles away in order to save money on printer ink. To be fair, her business *did* print many reports, and printer ink was a notable business expense. However, had she stopped to focus on which activities would have the most impact on her main goals, she might have found a more effective use of her time that would benefit her business even more than the money saved and time spent on driving so far for printer ink.

As the Operations Manager of your business, your two-part goal (on Tuesdays) is to first *review* all the necessary tasks that keep your business efficient and profitable (your main goal) and then *prioritize* them. Which of the many operational tasks is the most critical to your continued profits? Refer back to your business plan. What are your strategies? What are your objectives? What are your revenue goals? Which operational tasks will move you closer to your goals? Ensure the completion of these necessary action items by reserving time for them on your calendar.

If you are not the Operations Manager of your business, then meet with the person who fills that position. You need to review the current reality, reestablish the business vision and objectives, and agree on the important actions steps to commit to for the upcoming week. Before the meeting ends, establish the measurements for the result you expect and then schedule a time for next Tuesday's meeting.

If you are efficient and consistent from week to week, this meeting should not take more than a few minutes every Tuesday.

Wednesday Is Finance Day

Wednesday is the day to use your leadership time to look at the numbers. It is really a matter of comparing your current numbers with the revenue goals you set in the business-planning phase of the revenue modeling exercise.

This may include balancing the checkbook and/or entering other important data into your financial bookkeeping, but it is most likely to be a comparison of your actual weekly sales numbers against your projected revenues.

These numbers provide the information you need in order to set the direction for your marketing and sales efforts for the upcoming week. The numbers tell you exactly how you are doing and, as the leader, you will use this information to decide the most important task to take care of next.

Your strategic analysis of the current strength of your business will determine the topics of your upcoming meetings with your marketing and sales departments. Make sure your decisions are clear, measurable, and based on your current (and accurate) data. Then it is time for "meeting adjourned and everyone get back to work!"

Thursday Is Marketing Day

As a small business owner, you probably spend most of your time on marketing and sales because that is what increases your business profits. As the marketing representative of your company, it is your responsibility to know your customers well, very well. You should be the one who best understands the needs of your target market, and it is your job to build and maintain the reputation of your business as their supplier of choice.

So ... how do you know if you are doing your job well? You can gauge the health of your business by knowing how many new leads were generated last week, and projecting how many new leads you expect to generate this week. You are keeping track of leads, right?

The business objectives set in your business plan and revenue model depend on growing your customer base. You can only know if you are successful at building your business when you are counting your new leads and measuring them against the past. So, Thursday is Marketing Day—the day to count new leads.

How many inquiries have you had? Website page hits? Phone calls? Which of your marketing systems are working best for you and what needs to change?

With actual data at the forefront of your mind, you will be able to set some clear goals for the week ahead.

Friday Is Sales Meeting Day

We finally come to the most important goal of any business: making sales. Everything you have done in every staff meeting all week has been preparation to improve your sales. Your responsibility in Friday's sales meeting is to review the results of your sales process. Your sales process is (or should be) a consistent strategy to take the leads generated by the marketing department from inquiry to close. Your sales goals come from your revenue projections.

Sales are often a difficult challenge for the small business owner. If you discover that sales are not what they should be during this meeting, you need to use all of your resources to address the problem. Review the processes you have in place for any possible weak points.

Consider how each department can contribute to improving sales results. What is the quality of the leads brought in by your marketing efforts? Are they the right demographic? Do they have the resources they need in order to purchase your product? How about operations—are your current customers satisfied? Do they return to buy from you again? Are there any outstanding complaints that may point to a bigger problem?

Based on the information you gathered in your staff meetings throughout the week and as the leader of your own business, you are now prepared to make some strategic decisions about priorities for the upcoming week. Write down your thoughts and leave them on your desk for consideration by the CEO during your regular Monday morning meeting. At this, point it's "meeting adjourned—have a good weekend!"

Next Steps

You now have a clear plan and a process for enacting your plan every day of every week. With a clear focus, motivating goals, and accurate measurements, you will be able to choose your tasks each day in order to manage your time efficiently. That will, in turn, maximize the profitability of your business.

Module 9 Workbook—Action Planning: How to Do the Right Thing

Learning Objectives

- Demonstrate executive level leadership through continued planning.
- Develop a clear Action Plan for each important strategy.

For most emerging entrepreneurs, the action steps involved in business building are spontaneous and reactive. When one lacks a plan and instead merely reacts to circumstances, chaos quickly emerges. Managing chaos everyday has its emotional rewards; one feels busy and productive. However, busy and productive without a strategic objective is rarely profitable over the long term.

Exercise	How to be a CEO
Exercise	Create an Action Plan

Index to Exercises

How to Be a CEO

Schedule Time for Leadership

This exercise is so simple you may have already done it. If you have read Chapter 9, you have given some thought to the five important areas of your business. You understand that, as the leader of your business, it is your responsibility to lead, manage, and make decisions about each of these areas.

To assure that no important aspect of your business is neglected, take the time now to schedule (write it down in your calendar) weekly time to review your progress toward your strategic objectives in each of these areas:

- Planning
- Operations
- Finance
- Marketing
- Sales

How to Create an Action Plan

How to Do the Right Thing

Tasks are the stepping stones to meeting your objectives;
Objectives are the milestones of successful strategies.

An Action Plan is nothing more than a list of well-thought-out tasks. The key to a successful action plan is to tie it very specifically to your strategic plan. Without careful thought given to how your actions complete your strategies, chances are the actions you take each day will not be effective.

The Action Plan you create will guide your day-to-day activities. When done carefully the plan will include what needs to be done, when it needs to be done, who is responsible to do it, and what resources are necessary. The results or outputs of your actions should bring you ever closer to realizing your goals and ultimately your dreams.

How to Create an Action Plan

What Must Be Done

What is it you are planning to do? Refer back to the strategies you developed in Chapter 6 and the important milestones you established. The tasks in your action plan should be carefully targeted toward reaching your milestones. (Figure 9.1)

ACTION	RESOURCES	TIME	RESPONSIBLE	DEADLINE
Identify the steps needed to achieve your objective	What will you need to complete this task?	Time needed to complete this task	Who will complete this task?	By when?

Figure 9.1 Simple action plan

The Steps to Follow

Depending on the outcome you seek, you may have many possible paths to follow. For example, if your goal is to increase your database of warm leads, you may choose any number of marketing initiatives to accomplish this: e-mail campaigns, cold calling, sky writing, billboards, and so on. If you are not yet clear on the best method for realizing your desired outcomes, you may want to take some time to brainstorm possibilities before settling on the action that best fits your capacity, budget and philosophy.

Step One

Identify the Critical Steps

Once you have decided on a specific plan to implement your strategy, write down the critical steps to bring the outcome into reality. For complex projects it is useful to use small cards or notes. Use a wall or large table to cluster each step in sequence.

Step Two

Establish a Schedule for Completing Each Action

When you have sequenced your steps, you will see that some things need to happen before other things.

To the best of your ability, calculate how much time each step will require. Working backward from your desired date of completion, assign time frames to each step in the process.

This process will help you decide when an activity must begin and when it needs to be completed.

Step Three

Decide Who Is Responsible

In the beginning, you may work alone but, as you grow, you will (you must!) reach out for help. Assigning responsibility for the outcomes you require is the only way to assure that the work gets done. It is also the best way to manage your own leadership process. How will you monitor the performance of your staff? If you are not clear about the work they are to perform, how will they know what is required?

Step Four

Consider What Resources Are Needed

Consider these possible requirements: money, people, materials, services, and transport. Since money is likely to be your most guarded resource, estimate the money required to acquire the people, materials, services and transport you will need. Do this carefully. Many is the business that has struggled with projects that run over budget.

Step Five

Measure the Outputs

Outputs are those things that show the activities have successfully completed. Outputs should be measurable. If not measurable in specific numbers, then measurable in a concrete way. If you are struggling to come up with a measurement, ask yourself: how will I know, in an objective way, that this outcome is complete?

CHAPTER 10

Chaos Theory: Preparing for the Future

In chaos, there is fertility.

—Anaïs Nin

In this book, I have attempted to help you create order out of the creative chaos of your brilliant ideas, entrepreneurial ambitions, and the way things really are right now in this time and space of your life and business venture.

I hope that whatever feelings you had of confusion, discouragement, and/or loss of control have been organized into a plan for building a profitable business and a personal lifestyle of satisfaction.

If you have a level of confidence about what you need to do over the next few months (or years) in order to create your vision … congratulations! You have used your mind, brain, and thinking power to reinvent yourself. You've thought your way out of chaos, and in the process, you've created a businessperson with vision, leadership, and a plan.

However, a word of caution: do not get overly confident! Chaos inevitably returns as a system never stays organized for very long, and predictions are never completely reliable.

Imagine you are standing on the top of a very tall, very smooth mountain with a tennis ball in your hand. Now see yourself bending down and placing the ball at your feet. Let it go, and as the ball begins to roll, can you predict where it will stop? What are the chances the ball will end up in exactly the same spot every time?

That is a simple analogy of how the world works in general. Today you have a good solid plan for your business. Tomorrow you might get to work, but very small inputs (like being late for a meeting, hiring person "A" instead of person "B," and so on), may have very large and lasting effects on what happens in the future. That is a description of chaos, and chaos is the natural and creative state of the universe. Do not despair—embrace it!

We can never be sure how important our own individual contribution will be.

—Gandhi

Your Business Is a Dynamic System

A system is anything that is not chaos. Your business, as you now conceive it, is a system. And as a system, it is dynamic, it *will* change. You need to be prepared to adapt to that change. If you are too inflexible, if you rigidly stick to your plan, you will be unable to adapt to the inevitable changes and challenges in your marketplace. Conversely, if you are too relaxed, or if you fail to work your plan, your system will lose energy, fail to make money, and eventually cease to exist as a system.

Consider the buggy whip, Swiss analog watch, or rotary phone … even those innovative businesses that dominate our lives today (that is, Apple, Google, Facebook, and so on) will eventually be replaced. As an entrepreneur, you can never afford to become complacent. You can, however, learn to embrace the chaos as it occurs.

You must have chaos within you to give birth to a dancing star.
—Friedrich Nietzsche

When Founders Flounder: Letting Go

Steve Jobs was fired from his own innovative company. His story is so well known now that it has the mythical power of a legend. But Steve Jobs was not the first nor the last founder to flounder when it comes to sustaining a system they created.

If you plan to play the role of both founder and CEO of your business, you will need to dance with chaos. When you recognize the need for innovation, creative response, or opportunity—embrace it! But on a day-to-day basis, strive to maintain the organizing objectives of your business as they are laid out in your business plan. Work every day to establish sustainable profitability.

Now that you have a system, you may need to "let go and let others." If growth is your objective, there will come a time when you can no longer afford to be a lone wolf or the independent maverick. From a management perspective, realize that as your business grows you will no longer be able to do it all yourself. And if truth be told, you are probably not the right person for every aspect of your business anyway.

In a 2010 interview Peter O. Crisps, a venture capitalist familiar with the Rockefeller family (2010 interview for the Daily Beast), stated that Steve Jobs and the original Apple crew were very undisciplined—so much so that when invited to the Rockefeller home for dinner, they put Apple decals on the bathroom mirrors in the home. This is certainly not the behavior of a trustworthy leader.

The Apple Board fired Jobs in 1983. Since that time, the archetypal role of the eccentric founder has regained some respect to the extent that many companies choose to keep their founding geniuses on board once again. That is not to say, however, that they do not set boundaries and attempt to rein them in.

Once a system is up and running successfully, the important tasks often change from those of a founder to those of a manager. The skills of the original genius are no longer the skills needed to sustain the company. At this point, and especially if there are investors involved, the founder may find himself or herself in conflict with the board.

This potential for conflict is true for smaller family businesses as well as partnerships. When this happens, do not take it personally. Remind yourself that new skills are always needed as a company grows. For any good leader, it is a sign of success when you have led yourself right out of your job.

Of course, it is hard to let go of your creative accomplishment, and the transition can be very painful. Twenty-five years after Steve Jobs' dismissal, he still would not speak to the man Apple's board brought in as CEO in order to turn Apple around, who was also the man leading the move to fire Jobs.

If your company is small and you have no board or investors, it will be your job to know when other minds or skill sets are needed for the continued success of your business.

Honest Self-Appraisal

How well do you know yourself? What is your particular skill set? If you have not objectively explored the gifts you have, and more importantly, the gifts you lack, you will not be able to make a clear, unemotional decision about your own role in your growing company.

Know Your Challenges

Most of us believe we understand ourselves quite well, but most of us also believe that *other* people are clueless about the way *they* show up in the world. To be an effective leader, you need to be ruthlessly accurate about your own strengths and weaknesses.

The least expensive but most emotionally difficult way to learn about who you really are is to ask others to evaluate you.

Ask Them:

- How would you describe my leadership style?
- What should I stop doing to make me a better leader?
- If I could change one behavior in order to become a more effective leader, what would it be and why?

Listen to Them

Truly listening is the hardest part for most of us, and you must discipline yourself to listen without justifying yourself or defending your actions. Your reasons for your behavior are just your reasons. The valuable information you seek is how *others* see you, and how you can be a more effective business leader by changing your behavior ... just listen!

Based on what you learn from those you ask to be honest with you, choose one or two behaviors to work on. Observe yourself and notice when the targeted behavior surfaces and what circumstances trigger it. Make a plan to either stop or change that problematic behavior, then monitor and regularly review your progress.

Know Your Strengths

Working to improve one's weaknesses is not necessarily the most effective way to excel. Current thinking suggests it is more effective to work on building one's strengths instead of focusing on one's weaknesses, and it is certainly more rewarding to pursue one's gifts.

If you have the courage as well as the patience to complete one or more of the assessments found in Chapter 3, you will find the information valuable and perhaps even enlightening.

You may also choose to incorporate insights from a career counselor.

Build a Team

Once you know the gifts you bring to the table, ask yourself what other skills you need to grow your company into the vision you intend to create. If necessary, refer back to the vision statement and action plan you developed earlier in this book. Consider the important tasks to be completed in the near future—what skill set is needed to complete these tasks effectively? Which tasks are ongoing and might constitute an ongoing role?

Consider each area of your business including operations, sales, marketing, and finance. Who or what is needed to improve the results in each of those areas?

In the beginning, consider using freelancers and contract workers. You can find skilled experts in almost any area through an Internet search. You will also find almost every skill set has an association where you can access a directory of the members.

As the leader of your business, it is your responsibility to know enough about the job you are hiring for to provide clear expectations about roles, goals, and the price you are willing to pay. A good contract employee can be a long-term asset, so do not rush. Do your research and understand your requirements in order to find the right person for the job.

Next Steps

The ultimate goal of the business system you are creating is to release you from the system. When you sit down to compare your current reality with your vision at some point, you *will* find a match although it may not look exactly like you imagined it would. When I set a goal to live internationally, I envisioned Paris, but when the dust and chaos of relocation settled, I found myself in Johannesburg, South Africa. Still, as far as I was concerned, I had met the Commander's Intent of deeply experiencing another culture.

You will get caught up in the day-to-day task of building your vision. If you have planned carefully, the work you do will enhance your life, bring you joy, and provide a needed service to world. Then one day you will stop … look around … and realize you have created your vision. What will you do then?

Celebrate

Do not let this moment slip by unnoticed—celebrate it!

I have found that when I use this system, my visions indeed become reality. Nevertheless, all too often I am so busy living the lifestyle I created that I fail to notice the moment that should be celebrated.

Do not let this happen to you. When you find yourself wondering what is next, revisit your vision—the one you wrote at the beginning of this book—and acknowledge all that has come to pass for yourself as a result of your own hard work and leadership.

> *Celebration is an act of impressing (that) sadistic someone residing in you.*
>
> —Santosh Kalwar

Congratulate yourself on your accomplishments, then acknowledge *and express* your gratitude for the contribution of others.

Celebrate!

> *I celebrate myself, and sing myself.*
>
> —Walt Whitman

Module 10 Workbook—Chaos Theory: Preparing for the Future

Learning Objectives

- Reflect on what you have learned about yourself through your work with the materials in this workbook.
- Expand your self-awareness with on-going self-appraisal.
- Recognize your accomplishments and celebrate.

Thinking	Reflecting on learning
Self-awareness	Know thyself
Celebrate	Celebrate success

Index to Exercises

Reflecting on Learning

Reflecting on what you learned as you did the work of creative thinking, analyzing, assessing, and planning for your new business adventure is an important part of making what you have learned a part of your ongoing toolbox of skills, knowledge, and abilities.

Ask Yourself These Questions

Reflecting on the experience

- What did I learn?
- How did I learn it?
- How is this relevant?
- What else do I need to learn?

Reflecting on the implications

- How will I use this information?
- What will I find challenging?
- What is still missing?
- What new ideas have I developed?

Reflecting on "now what?"

- How will I use what I have learned?
- What will I do differently now?
- How will I share my learning?
- What are my new learning goals?

Self-Awareness: Know Thyself

He who knows others is wise, he who knows himself is enlightened.

—Lao Tzu

Do not cease learning about yourself. If all systems are dynamic and changing, you, too, are dynamic and constantly changing. Continue to learn about yourself in whatever way you choose: meditation, coaching, psychotherapy, assessments, peer review, and prayer. Set an objective now to continue to grow in self-understanding.

Any fool can know. The point is to understand.

—Albert Einstein

Finding the Help You Need

Beginning a business requires many different skills. Once you have a clear action plan and can determine the tasks necessary to complete your designated actions, you will be in a position to delegate.

When seeking a qualified person to delegate to, I recommend starting small. Hire temporary contactors with the skills you need. You will learn from them by the question they ask and when you find one that you work well with you can then consider hiring that person on a permanent or part-time basis.

To find people with the skill sets you need consider these following resources.

Local Networking Groups

In the age of social media, most independent service providers are eager to get in a room with those people—like you—who may need their services. And, who knows, they may need your service or product.

Get Out of the Office

Consider joining Business Networking International (BNI) if the other members seem like they dovetail nicely with your business demographic.

Explore *Meetup.com* online to see if there is a business networking group you can join or consider starting your own networking group.

Depending on the skill set you require, consider researching online the associated professional association. You will often find qualified professionals among the membership.

Here is a list to get you started but you will find more resources when you search for associations in your own country.

Hire Virtual Employees

In the beginning, you will need help but perhaps not full-time, daily help. For those time consuming, tedious or outside-your-skillset projects consider hiring a virtual employee or freelancer.

In *The Four-Hour Workweek*, author Tim Ferriss recommends "outsourcing life." You can try that if you want to but, in my opinion, it requires the same amount of leadership and planning to assign a virtual assistant in India the task of sending your mother a bouquet of flowers as it does to ask the same virtual assistant to develop a 1,000-name marketing database. Let the assistant do the business tasks so you will have the time you need to sincerely honor your mother. There are many outsourcing services for the savvy business leader. To begin, try these:

- UpWork
- 99 Designs

Alternatively, do a general search on outsourcing services in your local area and see what comes up.

Epilogue: Who Are You Now?

It is in vain to say human beings ought to be satisfied with tranquility.
They must have action, and they will make it if they cannot find it.

—Charlotte Brontë

One day you will stop, look around, and realize you have created your vision—you will celebrate success … then what?

Once you have succeeded at building your business, the question you must ask yourself is, "What is next?" If the creative fires of entrepreneurship are inspiring, you will want to do it again.

If so, start the business-building process by going through this book all over again. The experiences you have lived in the process of building your first (or most recent business) will have changed you. You will have grown, matured, and should have gained immeasurable wisdom. Your current reality is completely new, so start all over again. Create a new vision for yourself. Look around you at the world you now inhabit. Discover a new mission. Consider who you are now, and how this "new you" can contribute to the world.

The best way to predict the future is to invent it.

—Alan Kay

The great thing in this world is not so much where we stand, [but] in what direction we are moving.

—Oliver Wendell Holmes

The End… or Just the Beginning

About the Author

Dana K. Dwyer is an author, business coach, serial entrepreneur, and an expert in adult learning. Drawing on her years of experience building small businesses in the United States, Ecuador and South Africa, she has come to recognize that aspiring entrepreneurs need affordable support, reliable information and focused education if they hope to avoid the stress, discomfort and expense of figuring it out on their own. This book is intended to provide just that.

Index

OTHER TITLES IN THE ENTREPRENEURSHIP AND SMALL BUSINESS MANAGEMENT COLLECTION

Scott Shane, Case Western University, Editor

- *African American Entrepreneurs: Successes and Struggles of Entrepreneurs of Color in America* by Michelle Ingram Spain and J. Mark Munoz
- *How to Get Inside Someone's Mind and Stay There: The Small Business Owner's Guide to Content Marketing and Effective Message Creation* by Jacky Fitt
- *Profit: Plan for It, Get It—The Entrepreneurs Handbook* by H.R Hutter
- *Understanding the Family Business: Exploring the Differences Between Family and Nonfamily Businesses, Second Edition* by Keanon J. Alderson
- *Navigating Entrepreneurship: 11 Proven Keys to Success* by Larry Jacobson
- *Global Women in the Start-up World: Conversations in Silicon Valley* by Marta Zucker
- *Getting to Market With Your MVP: How to Achieve Small Business and Entrepreneur Success* by J.C. Baker

Announcing the Business Expert Press Digital Library

Concise e-books business students need for classroom and research

This book can also be purchased in an e-book collection by your library as

- a one-time purchase,
- that is owned forever,
- allows for simultaneous readers,
- has no restrictions on printing, and
- can be downloaded as PDFs from within the library community.

Our digital library collections are a great solution to beat the rising cost of textbooks. E-books can be loaded into their course management systems or onto students' e-book readers.
The **Business Expert Press** digital libraries are very affordable, with no obligation to buy in future years. For more information, please visit **www.businessexpertpress.com/librarians**. To set up a trial in the United States, please email **sales@businessexpertpress.com**.

CPSIA information can be obtained
at www.ICGtesting.com
Printed in the USA
BVHW091218160222
629130BV00004B/12